1.95

Top Dog
by
Mike Peters

TOR

A TOM DOHERTY ASSOCIATES BOOK
NEW YORK

This is a work of fiction. All the characters and events portrayed in this book are fictitious, and any resemblance to real people or events is purely coincidental.

MOTHER GOOSE AND GRIMM: TOP DOG

A Tor Book
Published by Tom Doherty Associates, Inc.
49 West 24th Street
New York, N.Y. 10010

ISBN: 0-812-51511-0

First Tor edition: September 1991

Printed in the United States of America

0 9 8 7 6 5 4 3 2

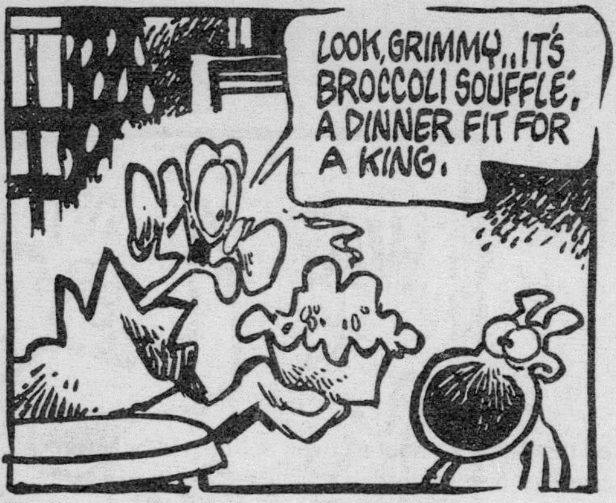
LOOK, GRIMMY... IT'S BROCCOLI SOUFFLE', A DINNER FIT FOR A KING.

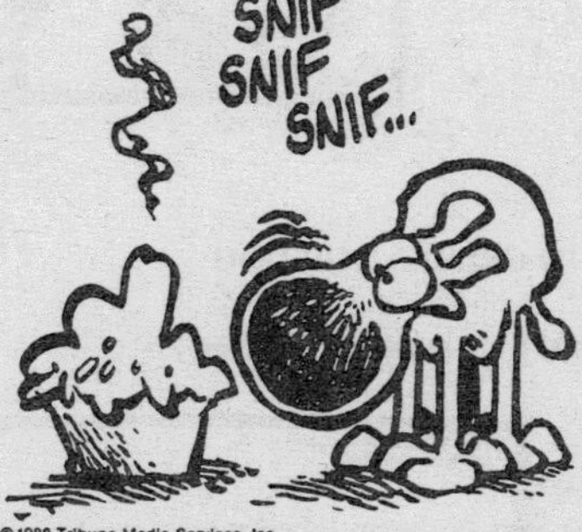
SNIF
SNIF
SNIF...

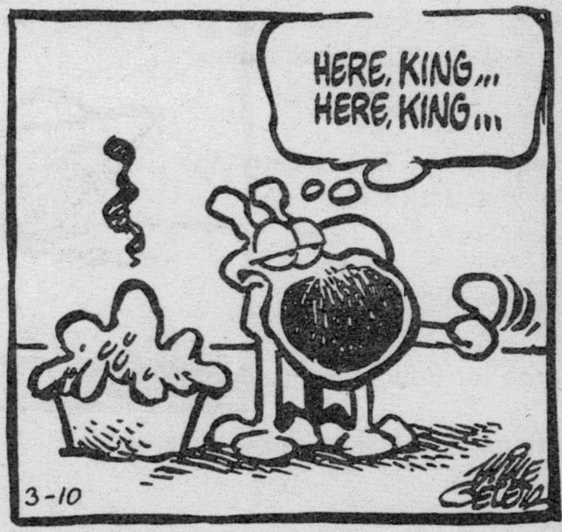
HERE, KING... HERE, KING...
3-10

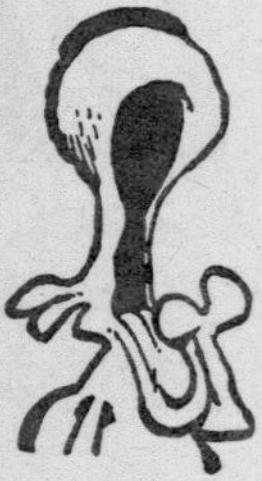

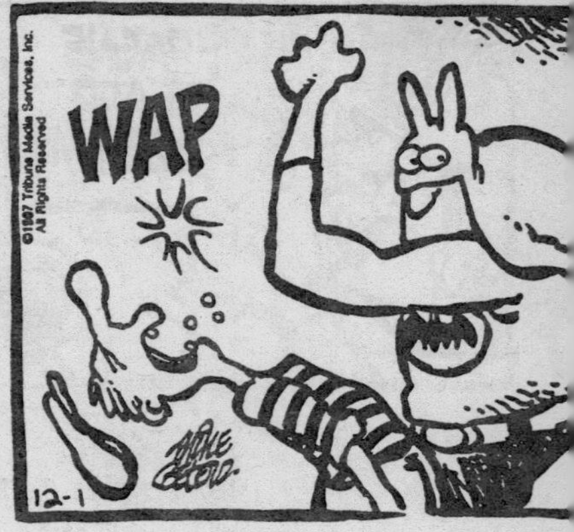
©1987 Tribune Media Services, Inc.
All Rights Reserved
WAP
12-1

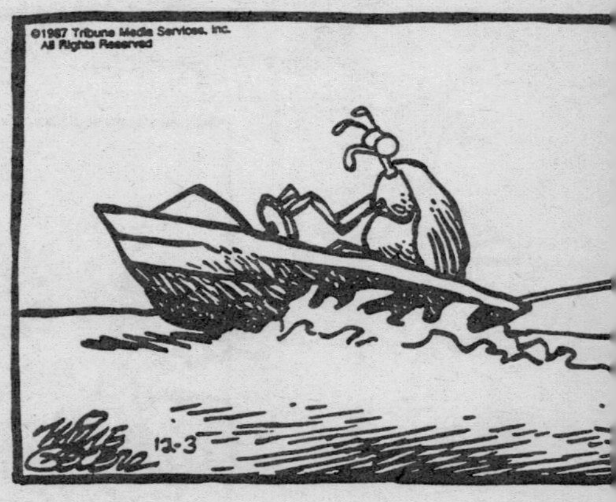
©1987 Tribune Media Services, Inc.
All Rights Reserved
12-3

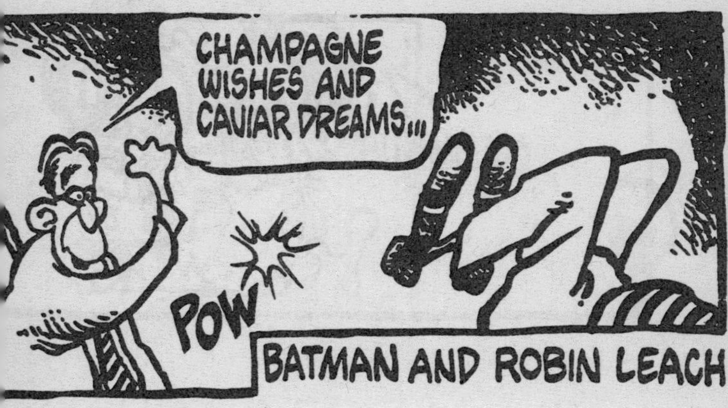
CHAMPAGNE WISHES AND CAVIAR DREAMS...
POW
BATMAN AND ROBIN LEACH

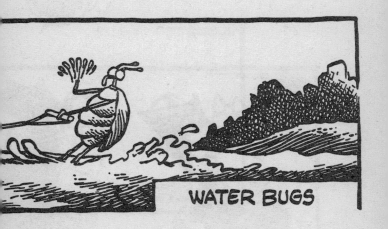

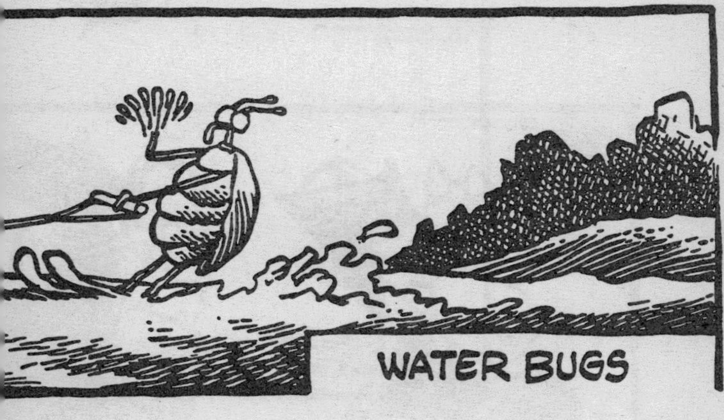
WATER BUGS

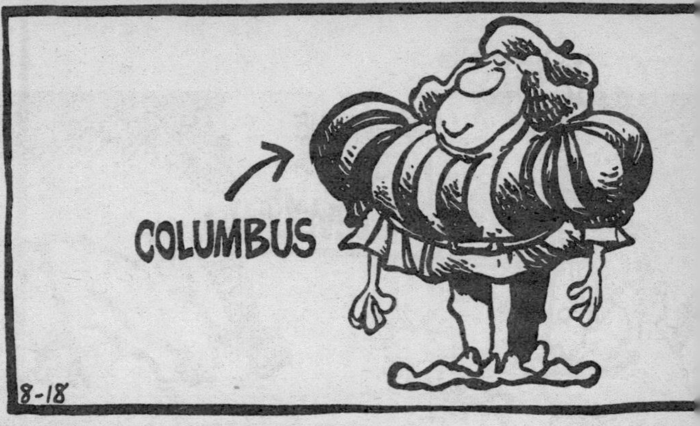
COLUMBUS
8-18

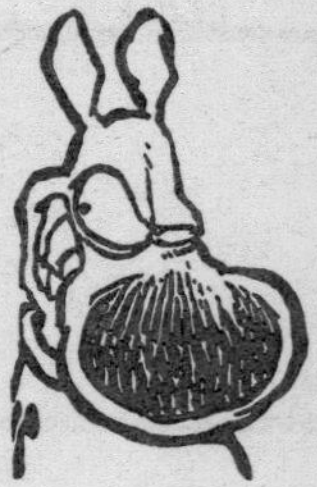

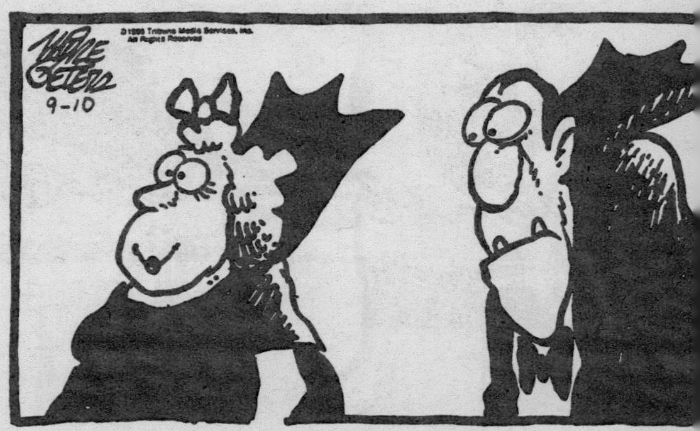
9-10

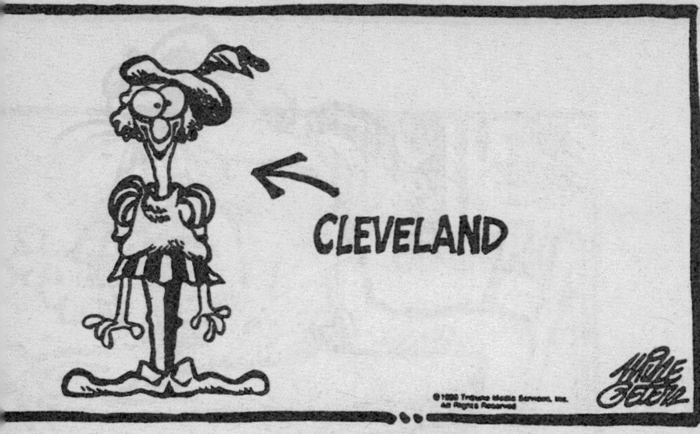
CLEVELAND

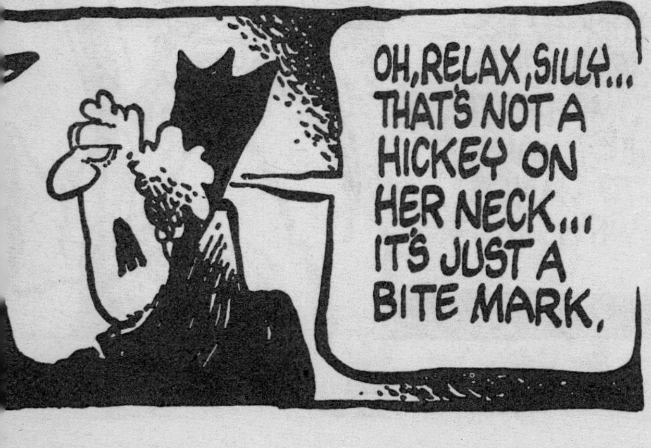
OH, RELAX, SILLY... THAT'S NOT A HICKEY ON HER NECK... IT'S JUST A BITE MARK.

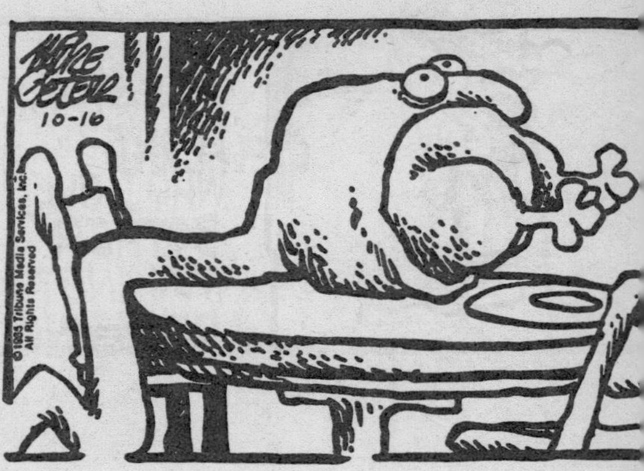
10-16
©1993 Tribune Media Services, Inc.
All Rights Reserved

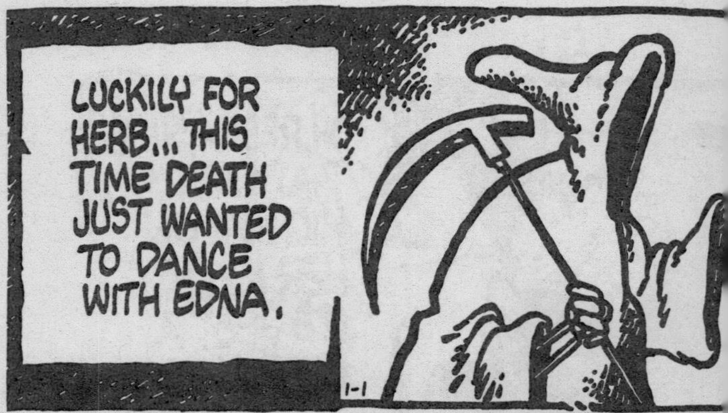
LUCKILY FOR HERB... THIS TIME DEATH JUST WANTED TO DANCE WITH EDNA.
1-1

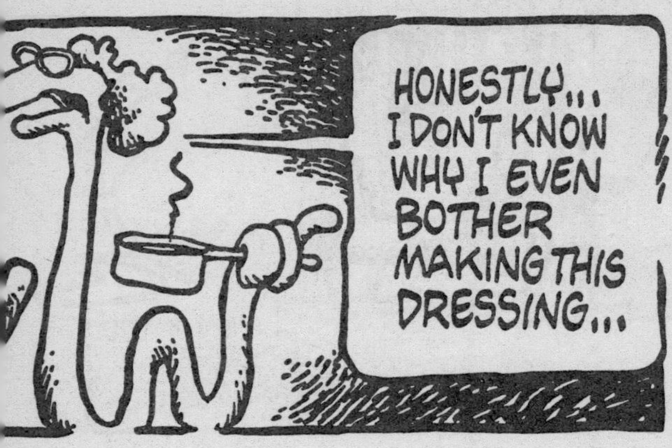
HONESTLY... I DON'T KNOW WHY I EVEN BOTHER MAKING THIS DRESSING...

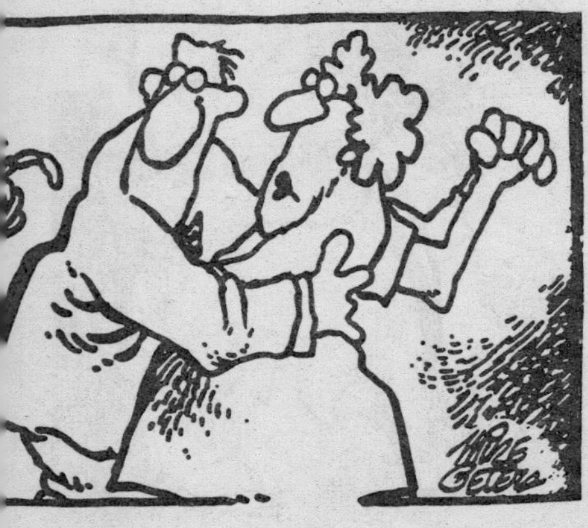

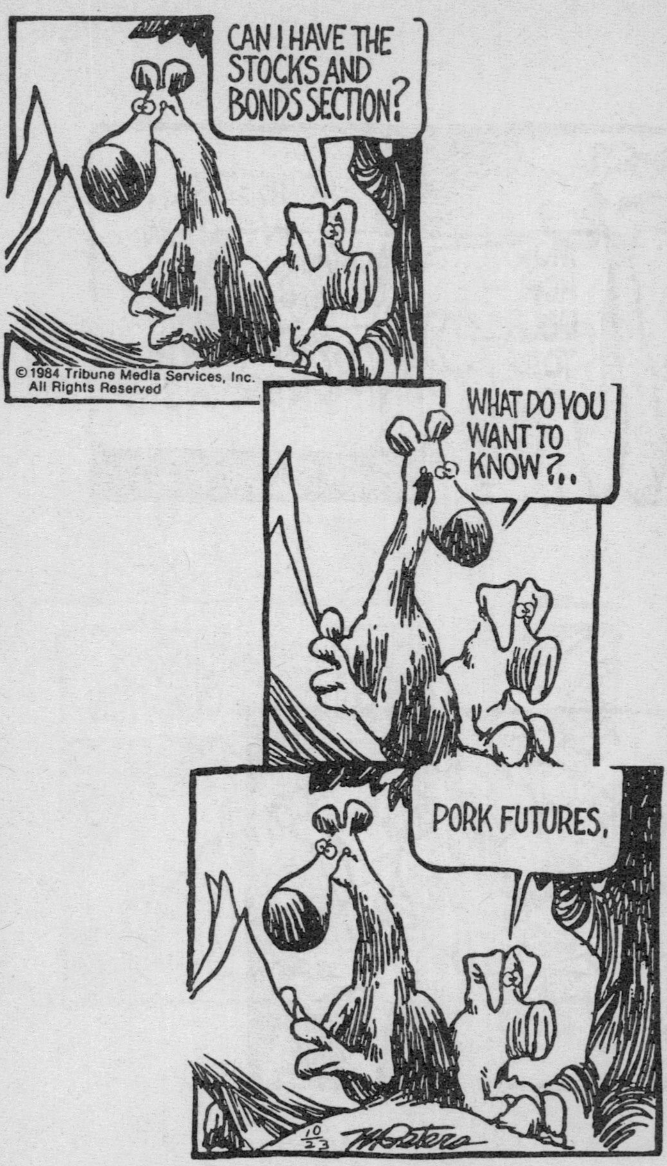
CAN I HAVE THE STOCKS AND BONDS SECTION?
© 1984 Tribune Media Services, Inc. All Rights Reserved
WHAT DO YOU WANT TO KNOW?..
PORK FUTURES.
10/23
M. Peters

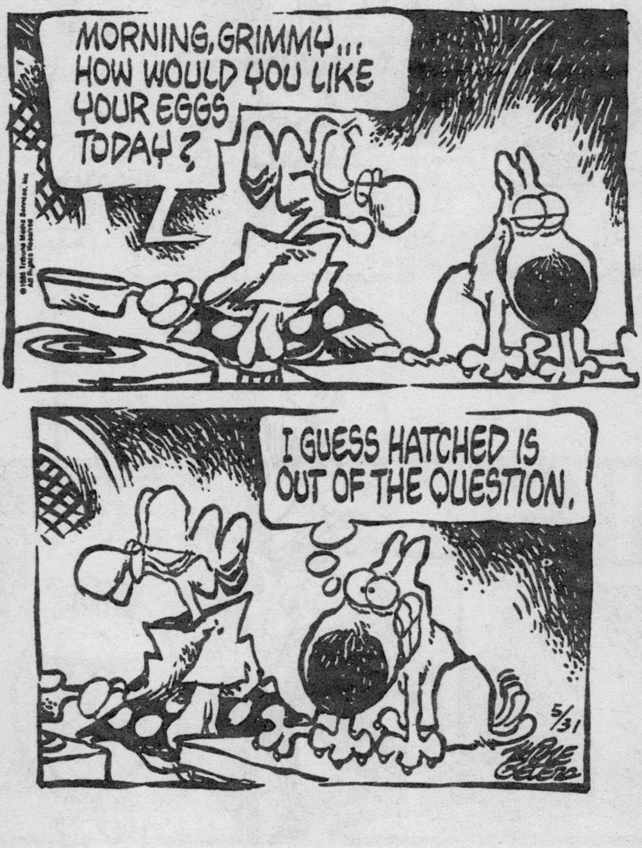
MORNING, GRIMMY... HOW WOULD YOU LIKE YOUR EGGS TODAY?
I GUESS HATCHED IS OUT OF THE QUESTION.
5/31

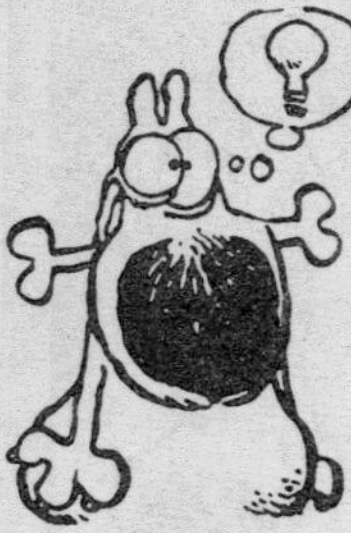

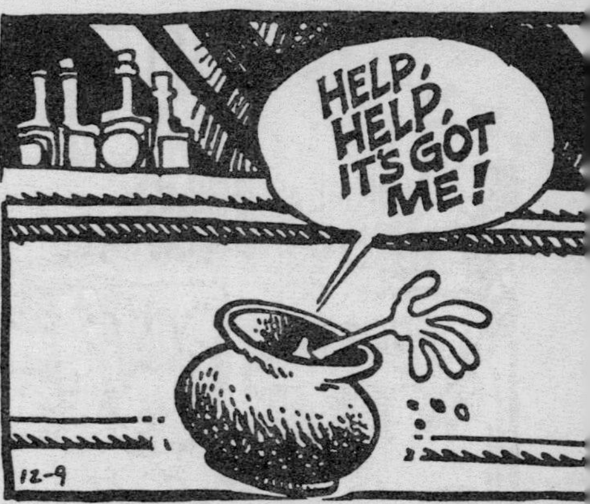
HELP, HELP, IT'S GOT ME!
12-9

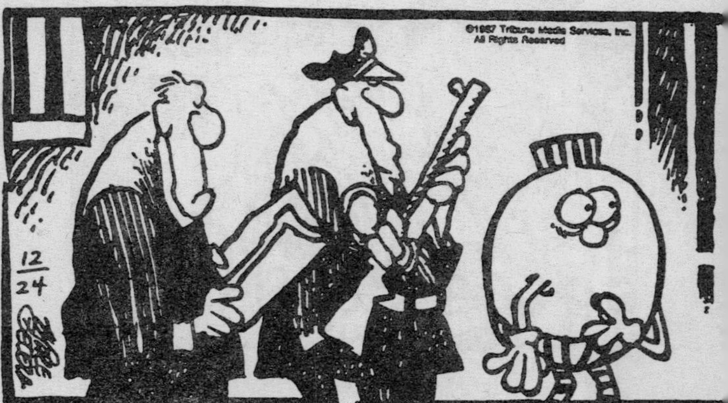
©1987 Tribune Media Services, Inc.
All Rights Reserved
12/24

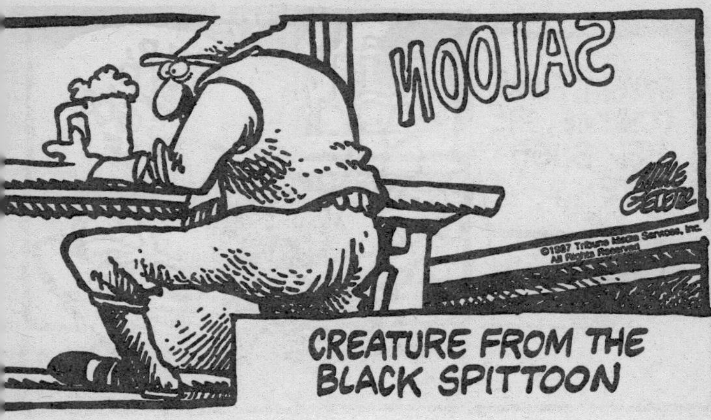
SALOON
©1987 Tribune Media Services, Inc.
All Rights Reserved
CREATURE FROM THE BLACK SPITTOON

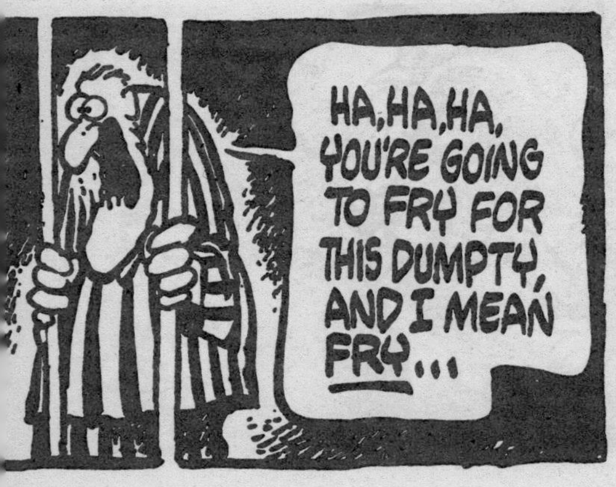
HA,HA,HA, YOU'RE GOING TO FRY FOR THIS DUMPTY, AND I MEAN FRY...

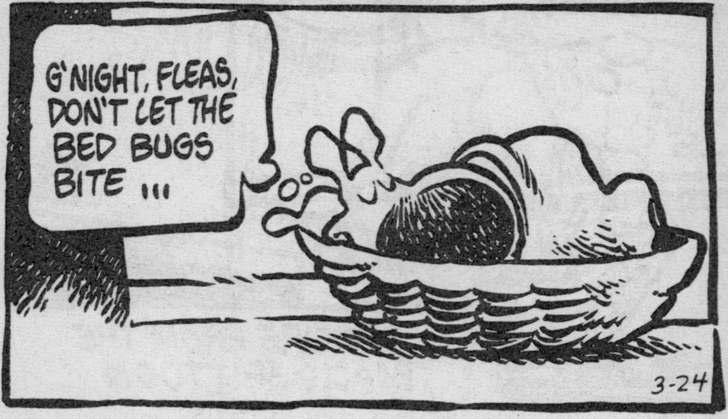
G'NIGHT, FLEAS, DON'T LET THE BED BUGS BITE ...
3-24

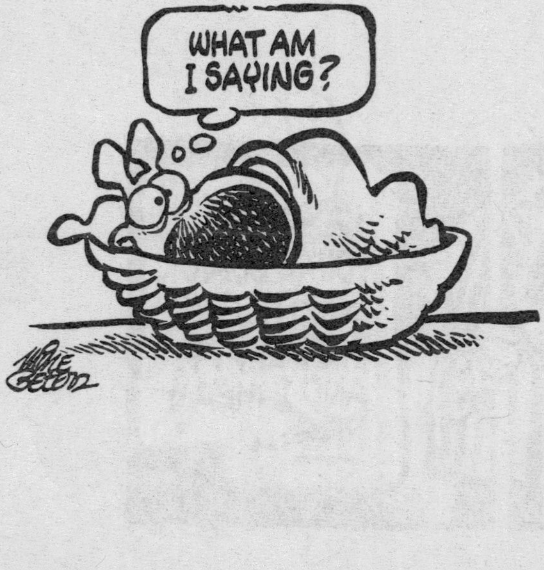
WHAT AM I SAYING?

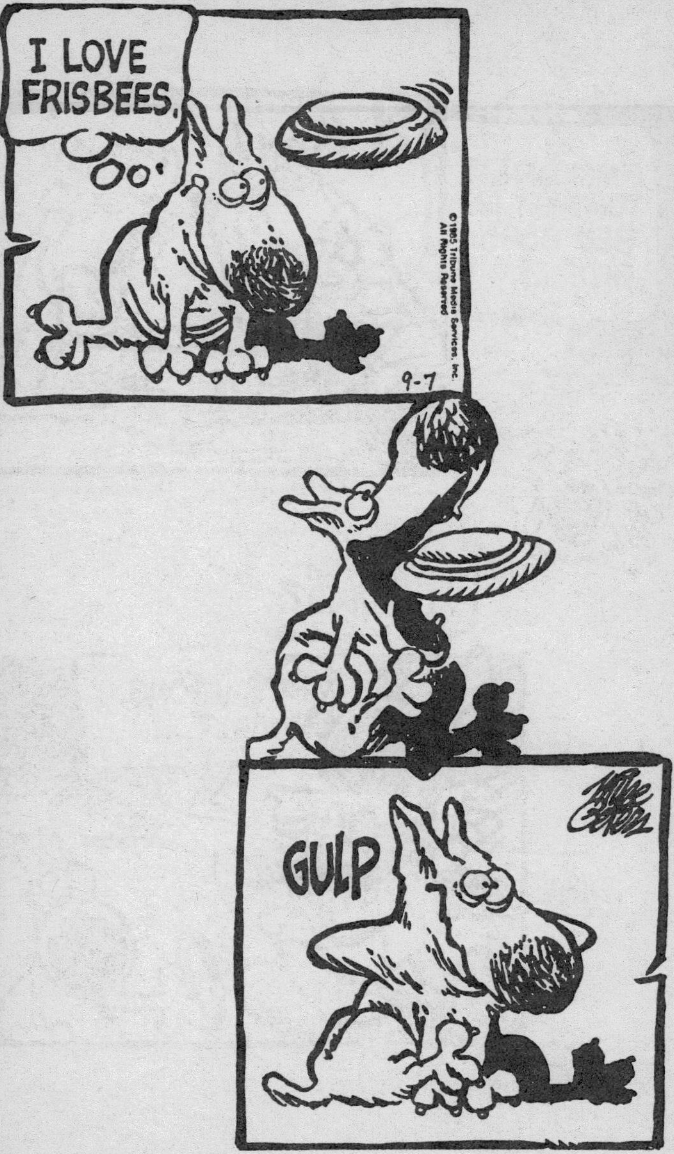

I LOVE FRISBEES.
©1985 Tribune Media Services, Inc. All Rights Reserved
9-7
GULP

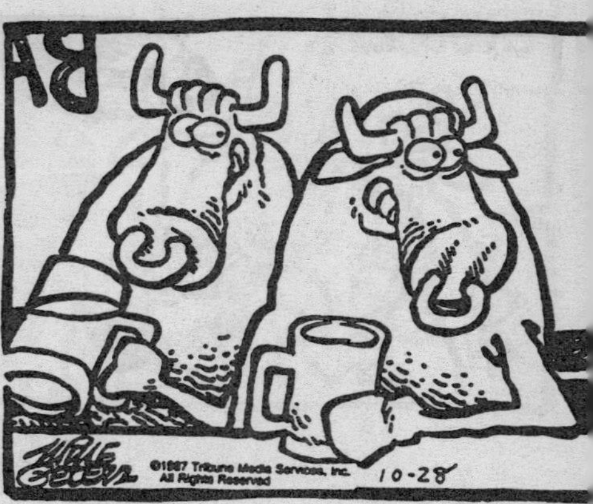
©1987 Tribune Media Services, Inc.
All Rights Reserved
10-28

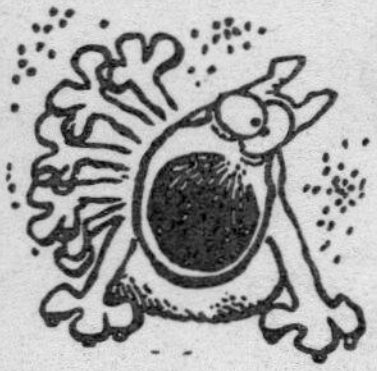

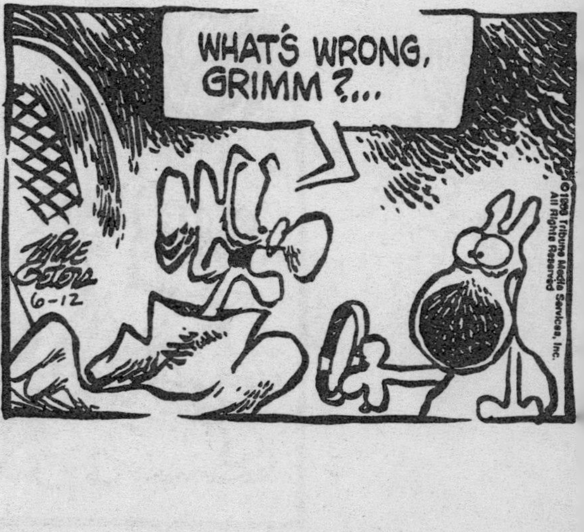
WHAT'S WRONG,
GRIMM?...
6-12

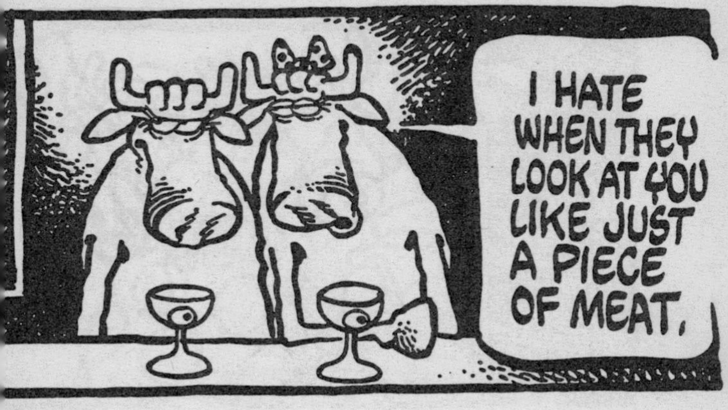
I HATE WHEN THEY LOOK AT YOU LIKE JUST A PIECE OF MEAT.

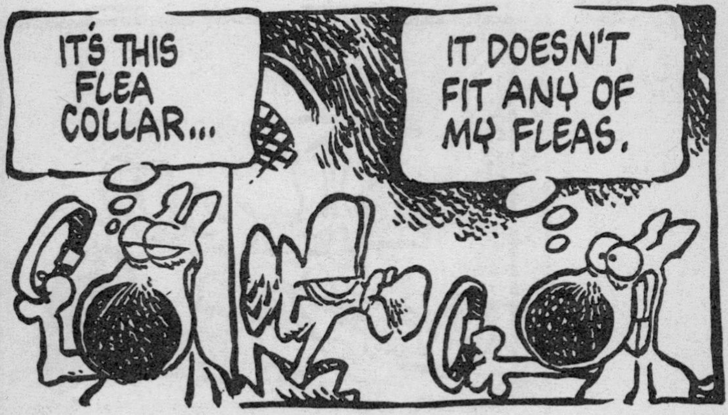
IT'S THIS FLEA COLLAR...
IT DOESN'T FIT ANY OF MY FLEAS.

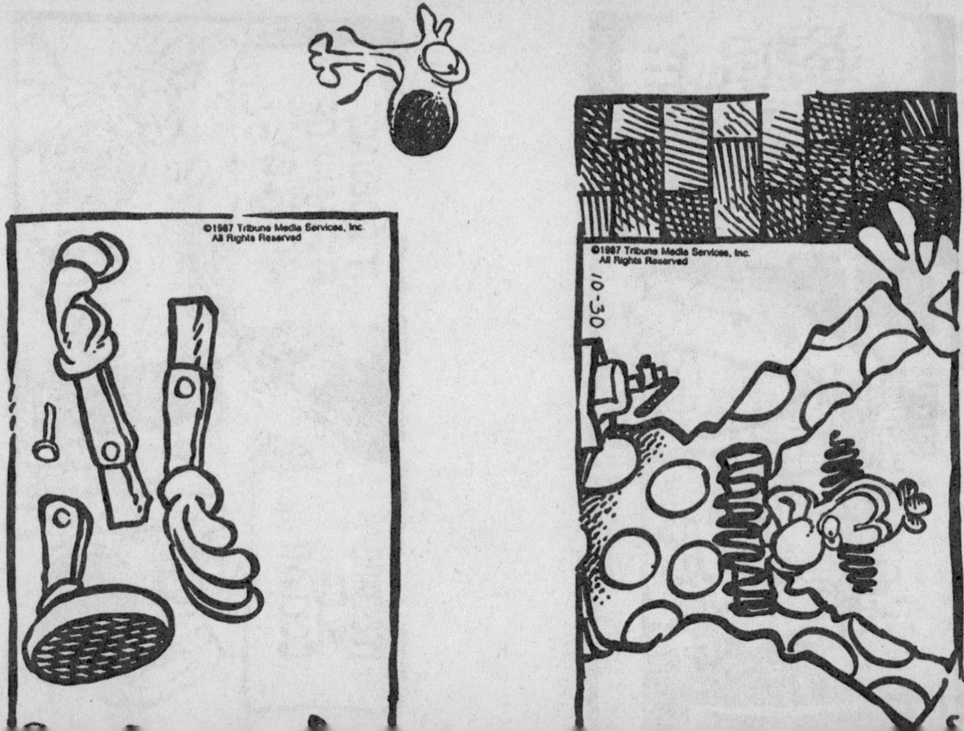
©1987 Tribune Media Services, Inc.
All Rights Reserved
©1987 Tribune Media Services, Inc.
All Rights Reserved
10-30

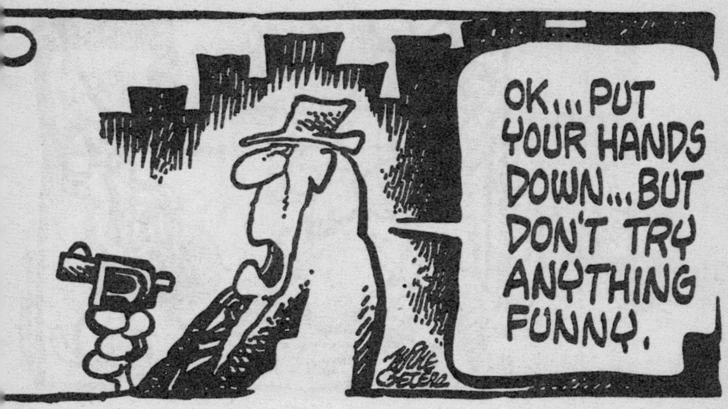
OK... PUT YOUR HANDS DOWN... BUT DON'T TRY ANYTHING FUNNY.

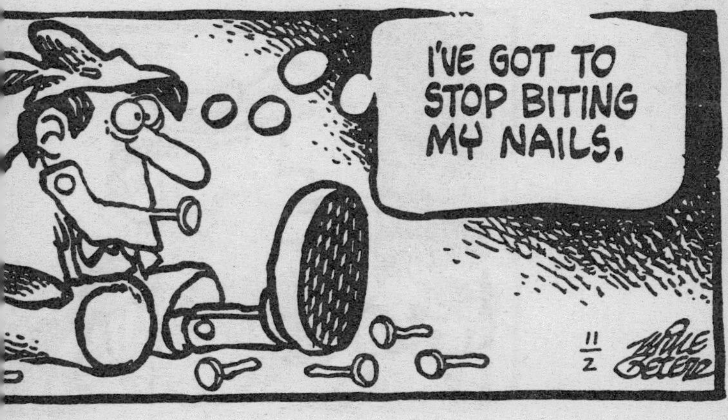
I'VE GOT TO STOP BITING MY NAILS.
11/2

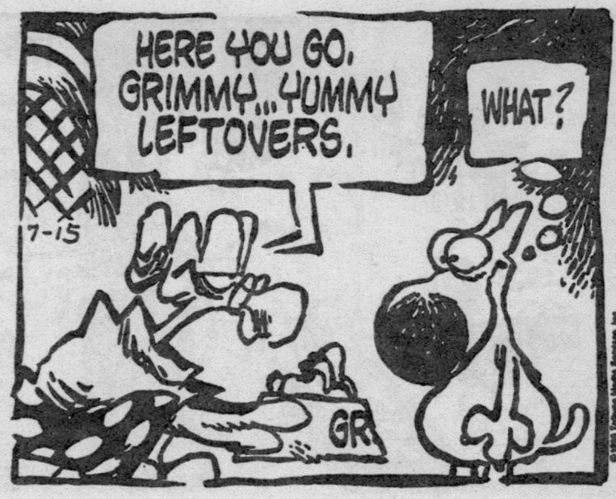
HERE YOU GO, GRIMMY... YUMMY LEFTOVERS.
WHAT?
7-15
GR

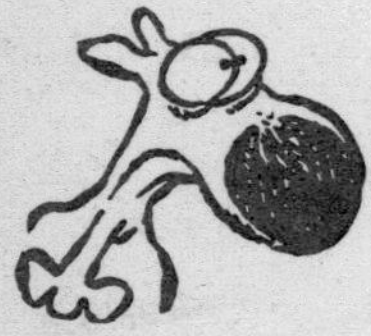

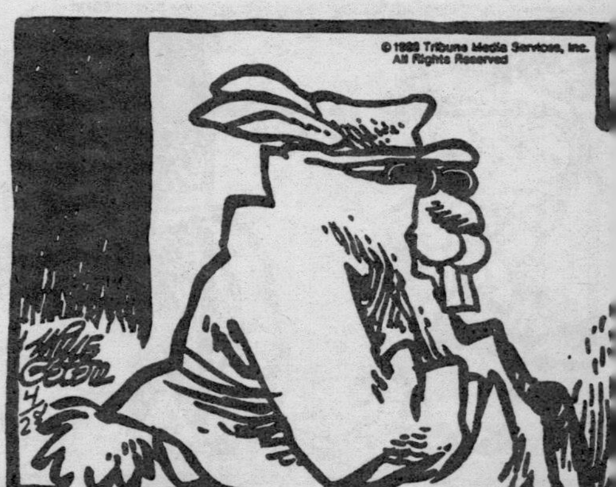
Tribune Media Services, Inc.
All Rights Reserved

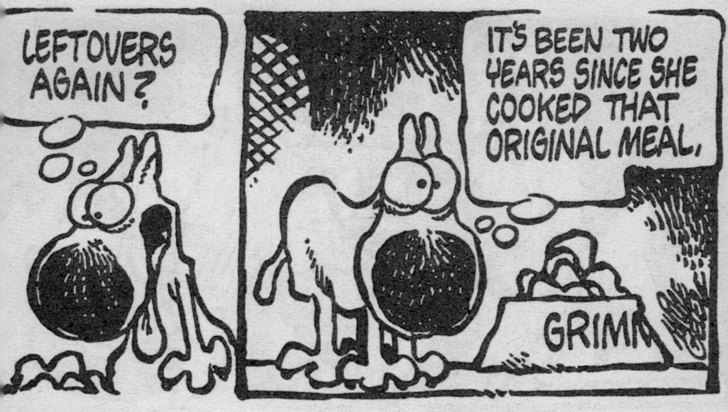
LEFTOVERS AGAIN?
IT'S BEEN TWO YEARS SINCE SHE COOKED THAT ORIGINAL MEAL.
GRIM

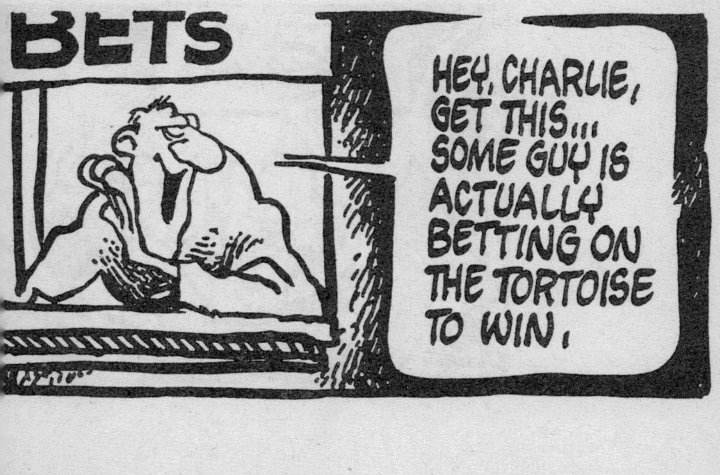
BETS
HEY, CHARLIE, GET THIS... SOME GUY IS ACTUALLY BETTING ON THE TORTOISE TO WIN.

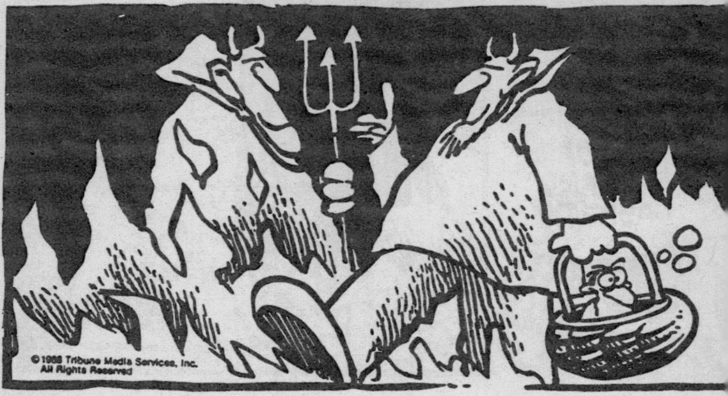
©1988 Tribune Media Services, Inc.
All Rights Reserved

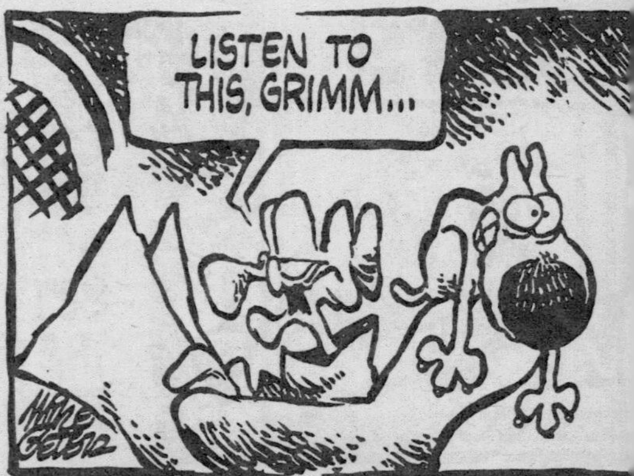
LISTEN TO
THIS, GRIMM...

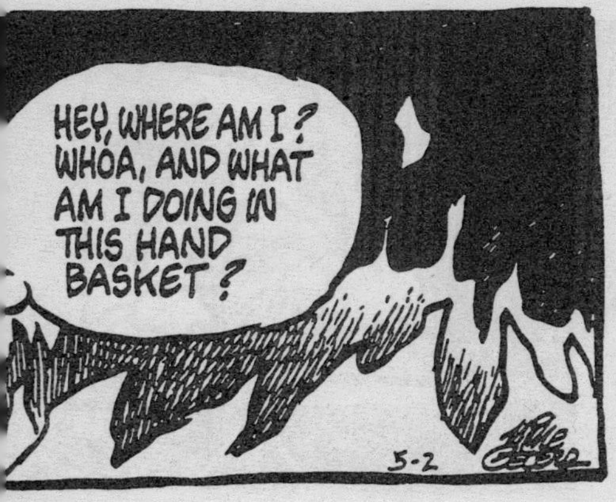
HEY, WHERE AM I? WHOA, AND WHAT AM I DOING IN THIS HAND BASKET?
5-2

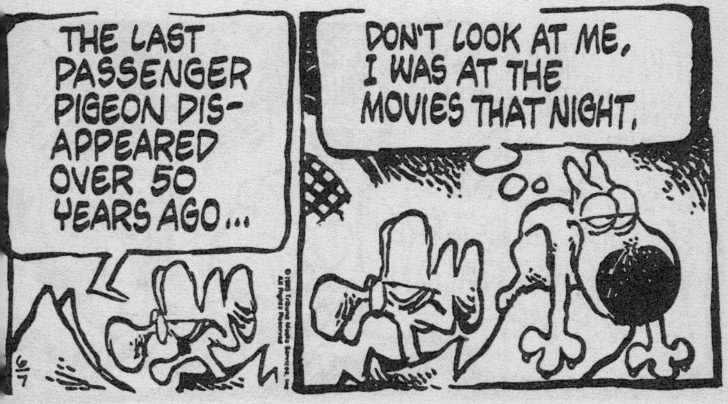
THE LAST PASSENGER PIGEON DIS-APPEARED OVER 50 YEARS AGO...
DON'T LOOK AT ME. I WAS AT THE MOVIES THAT NIGHT.

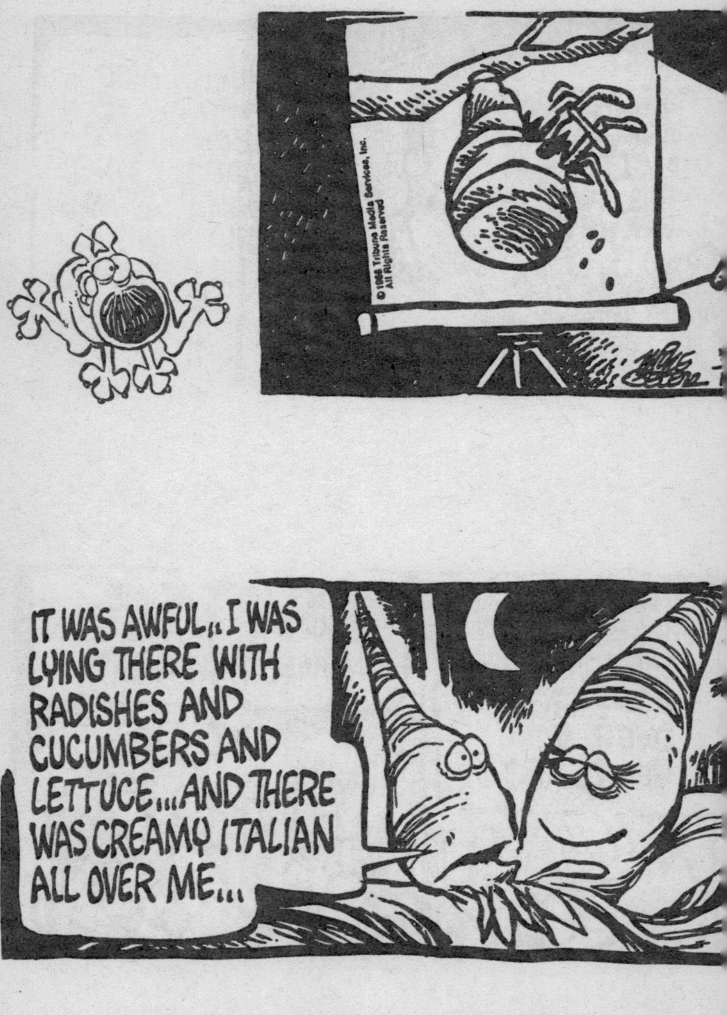
© 1988 Tribune Media Services, Inc. All Rights Reserved
IT WAS AWFUL.. I WAS LYING THERE WITH RADISHES AND CUCUMBERS AND LETTUCE...AND THERE WAS CREAMY ITALIAN ALL OVER ME...

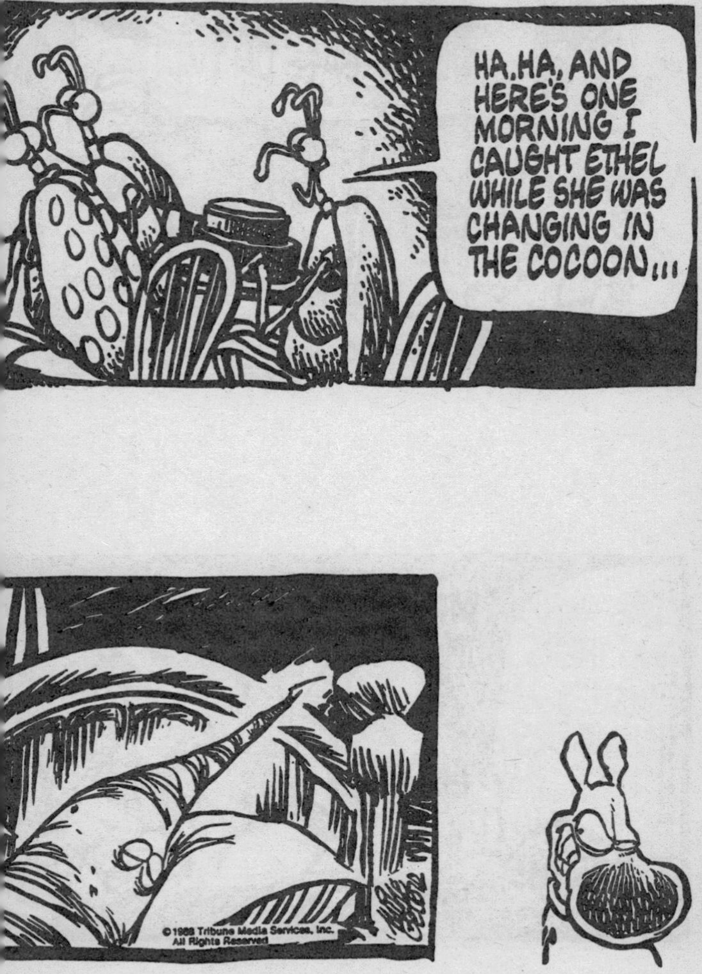
HA,HA, AND HERE'S ONE MORNING I CAUGHT ETHEL WHILE SHE WAS CHANGING IN THE COCOON...
© 1988 Tribune Media Services, Inc. All Rights Reserved

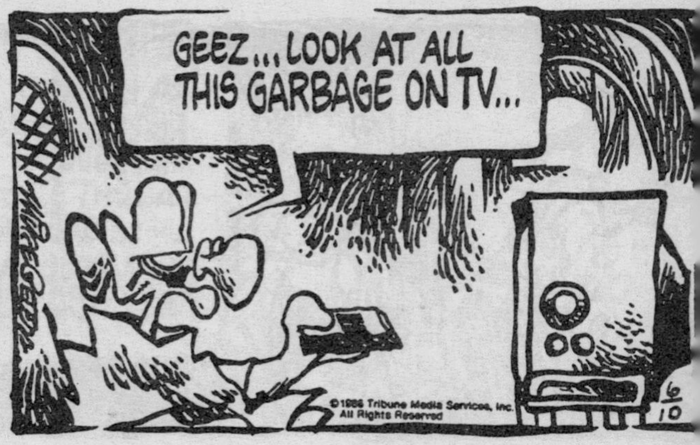
GEEZ... LOOK AT ALL THIS GARBAGE ON TV...
©1986 Tribune Media Services, Inc. All Rights Reserved
6/10

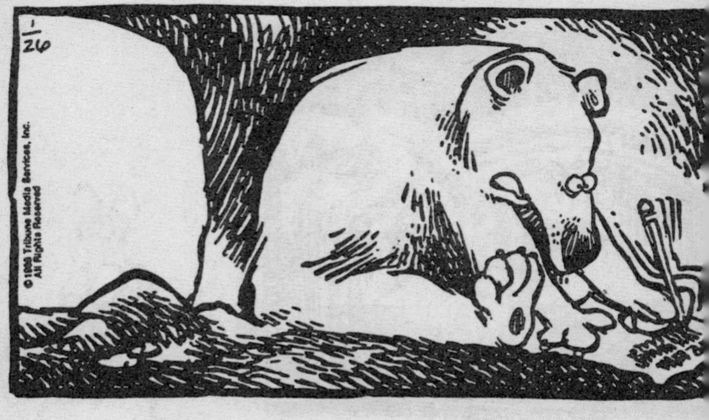
1/26
©1986 Tribune Media Services, Inc. All Rights Reserved

DER ABBY,
IS IT OK TO
HIBERNATE ON
THE FIRST DATE?

© 1988 Tribune Media Services, Inc
All Rights Reserved
2-17

12-25

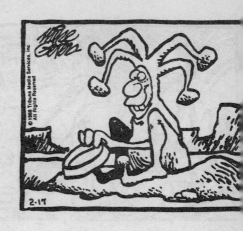

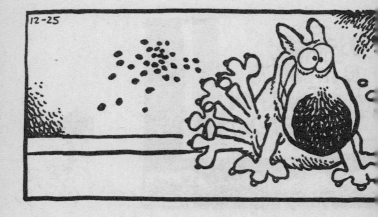

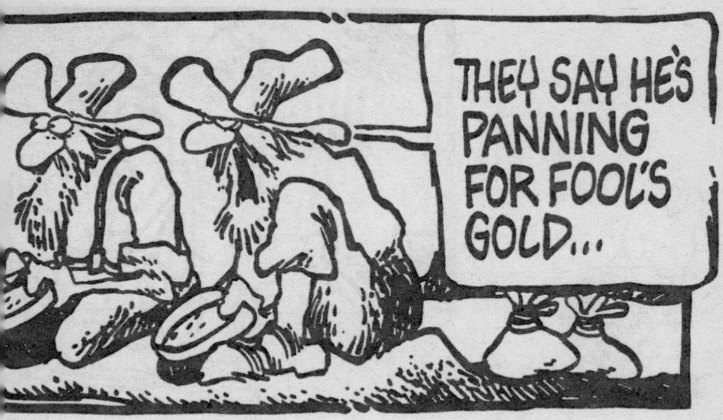
THEY SAY HE'S PANNING FOR FOOL'S GOLD...

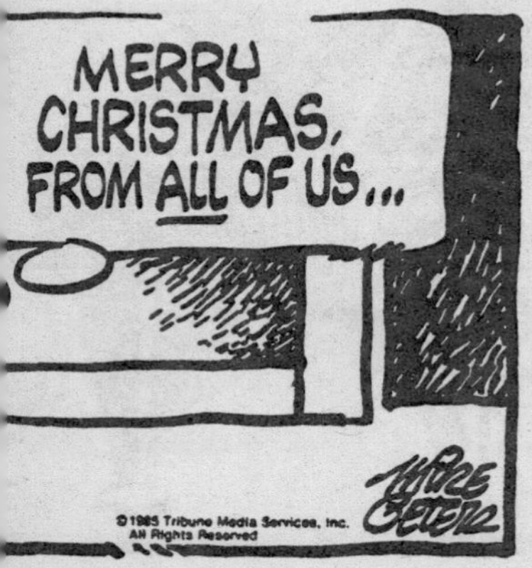
MERRY CHRISTMAS, FROM ALL OF US...
©1985 Tribune Media Services, Inc.
All Rights Reserved

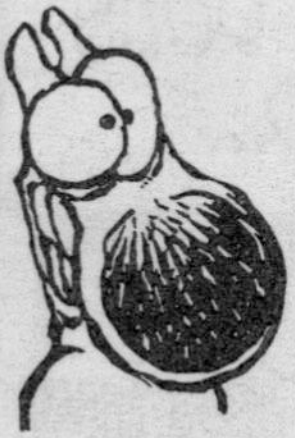

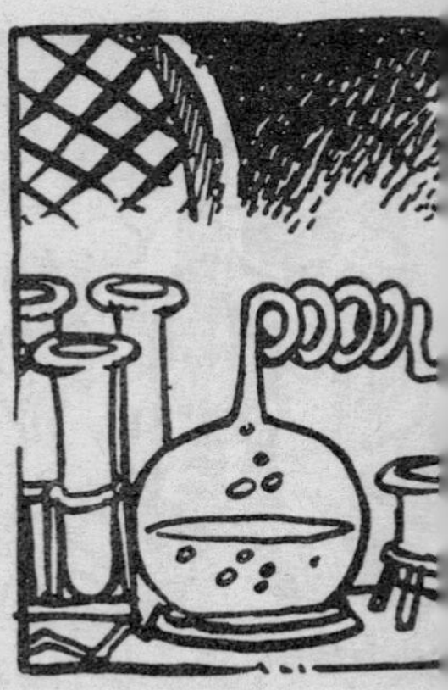

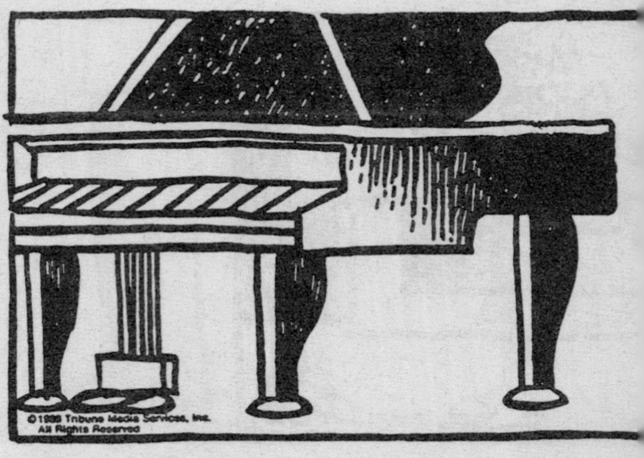
©1988 Tribune Media Services, Inc.
All Rights Reserved

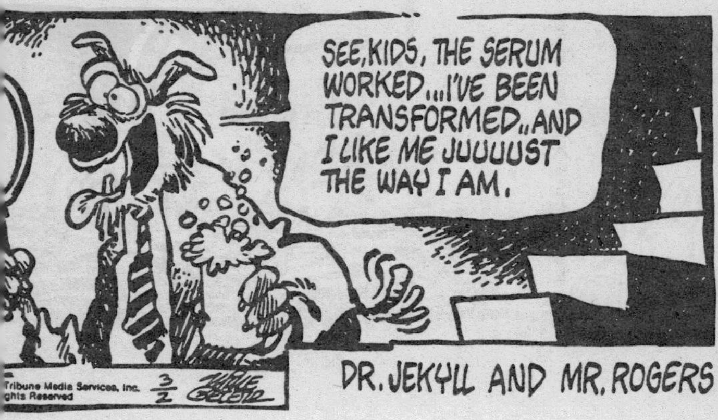
SEE, KIDS, THE SERUM WORKED...I'VE BEEN TRANSFORMED.. AND I LIKE ME JUUUUST THE WAY I AM.
Tribune Media Services, Inc.
ghts Reserved
3/2

DR. JEKYLL AND MR. ROGERS

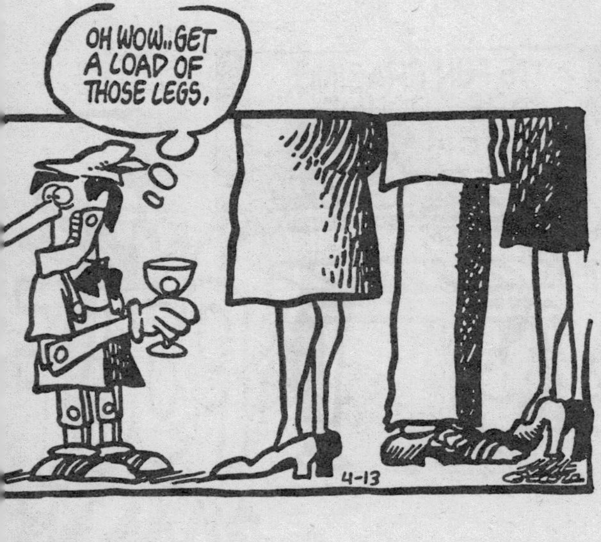
OH WOW.. GET A LOAD OF THOSE LEGS.
4-13

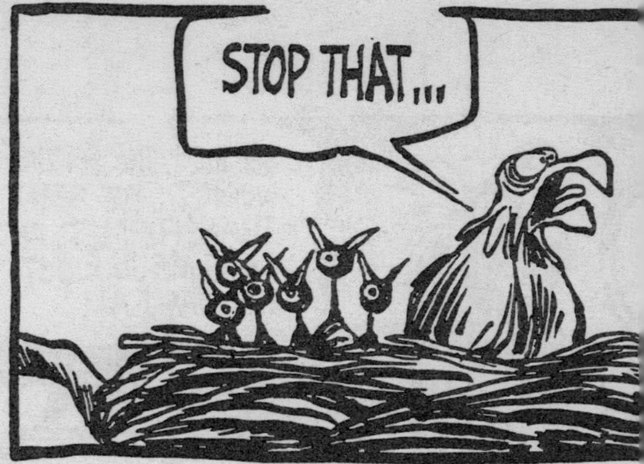
STOP THAT...

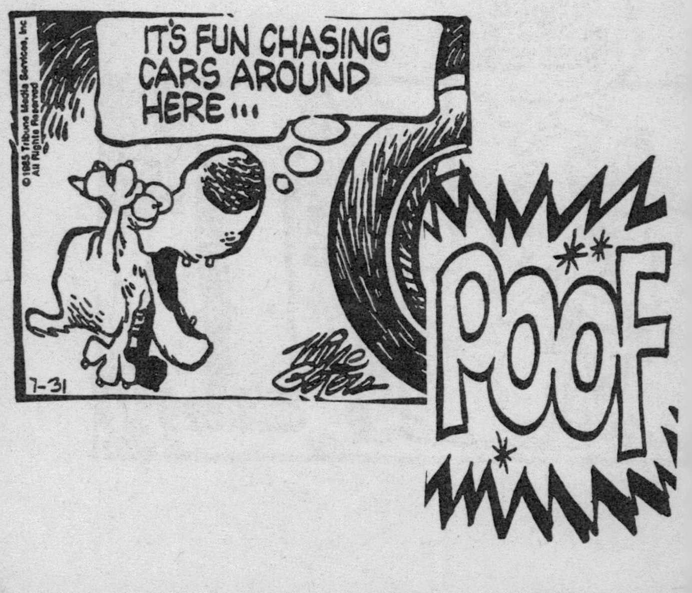
IT'S FUN CHASING CARS AROUND HERE...
© 1985 Tribune Media Services, Inc All Rights Reserved
7-31
POOF

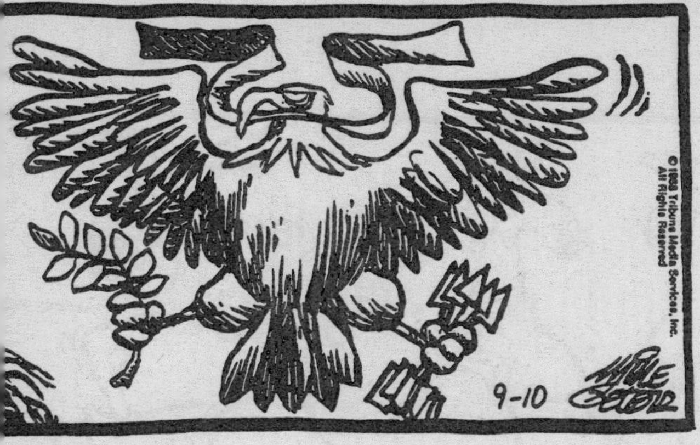
© 1988 Tribune Media Services, Inc.
All Rights Reserved
9-10
MIKE PETERS

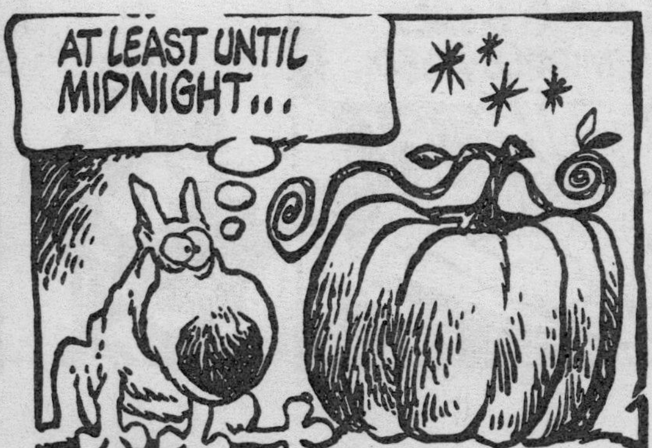
AT LEAST UNTIL MIDNIGHT...

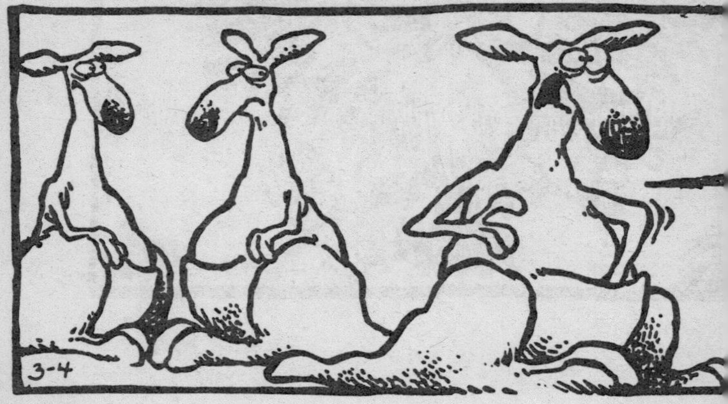
3-4

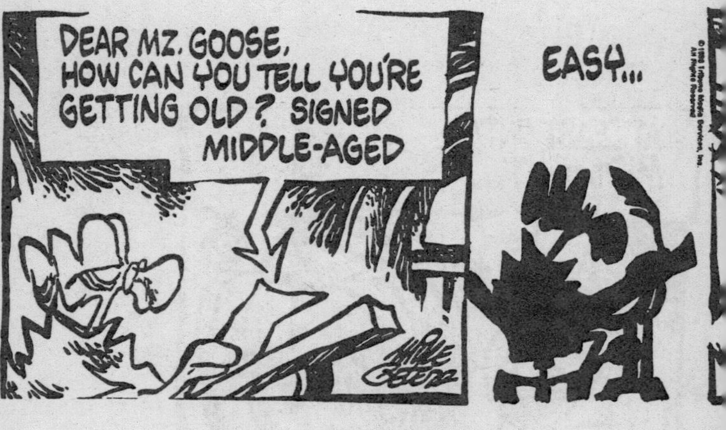
DEAR MZ. GOOSE,
HOW CAN YOU TELL YOU'RE GETTING OLD? SIGNED MIDDLE-AGED
EASY...
© Tribune Media Services, Inc. All Rights Reserved

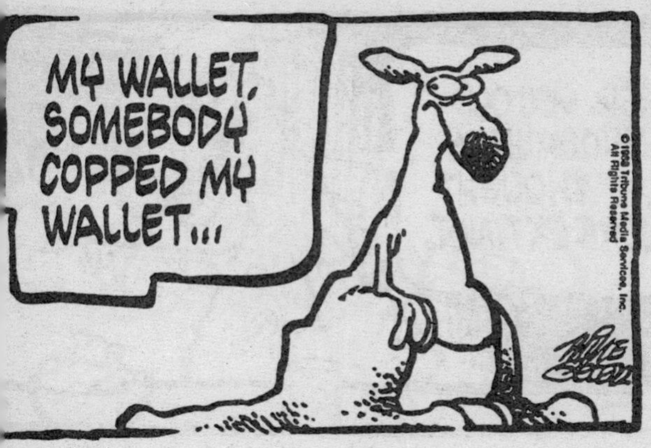
MY WALLET. SOMEBODY COPPED MY WALLET...
Tribune Media Services, Inc.
All Rights Reserved

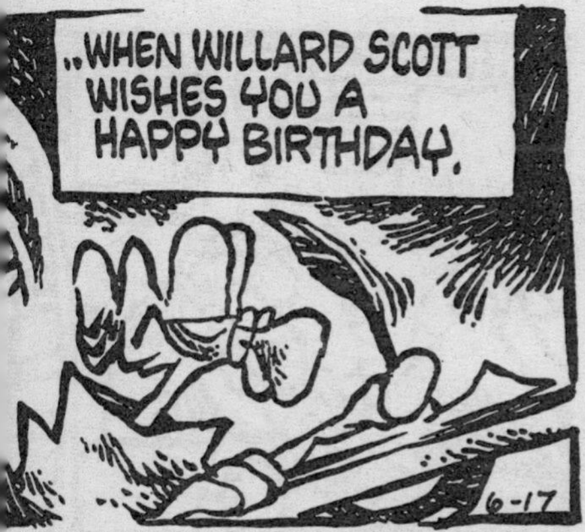
..WHEN WILLARD SCOTT WISHES YOU A HAPPY BIRTHDAY.
6-17

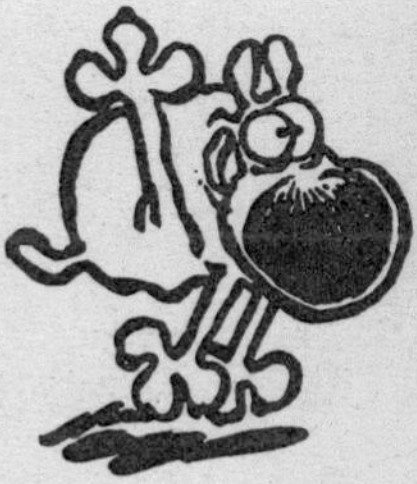

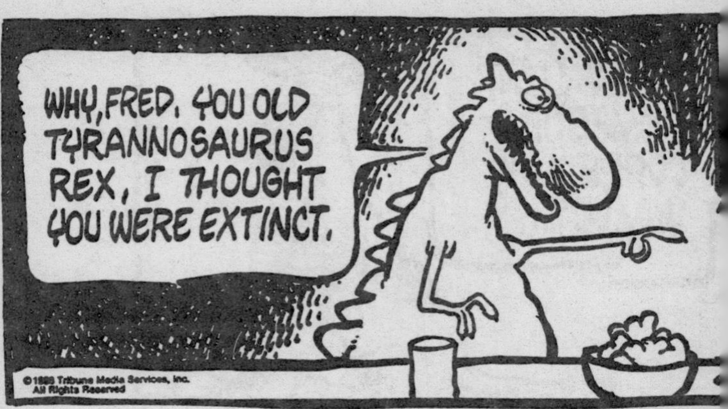
WHY, FRED. YOU OLD TYRANNOSAURUS REX, I THOUGHT YOU WERE EXTINCT.
©1988 Tribune Media Services, Inc. All Rights Reserved

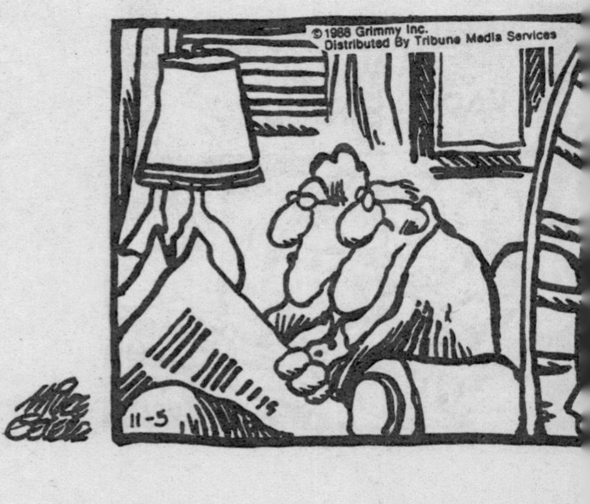
©1988 Grimmy Inc. Distributed By Tribune Media Services
11-5

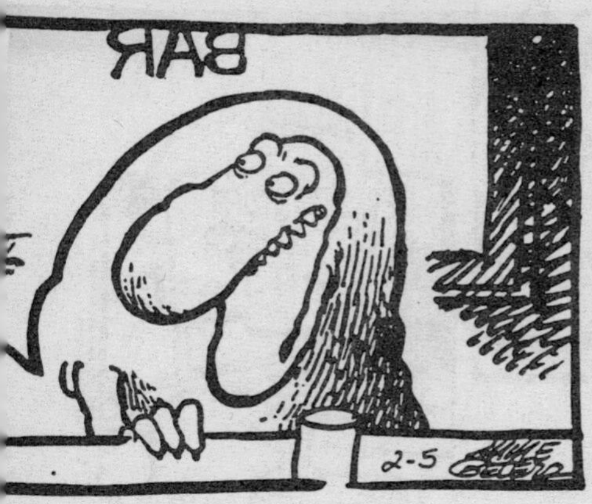
BAR
2-5

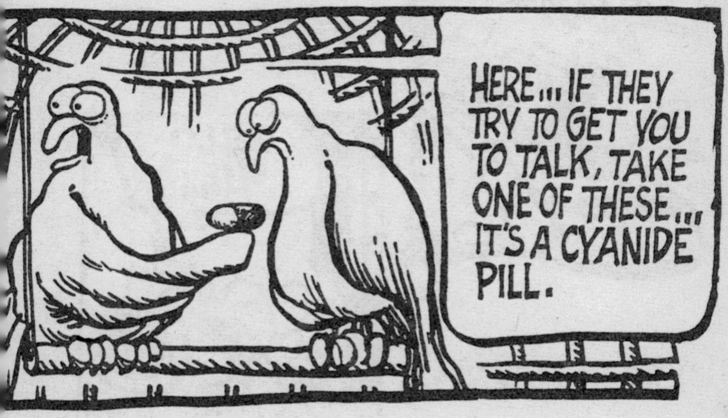
HERE... IF THEY TRY TO GET YOU TO TALK, TAKE ONE OF THESE... IT'S A CYANIDE PILL.

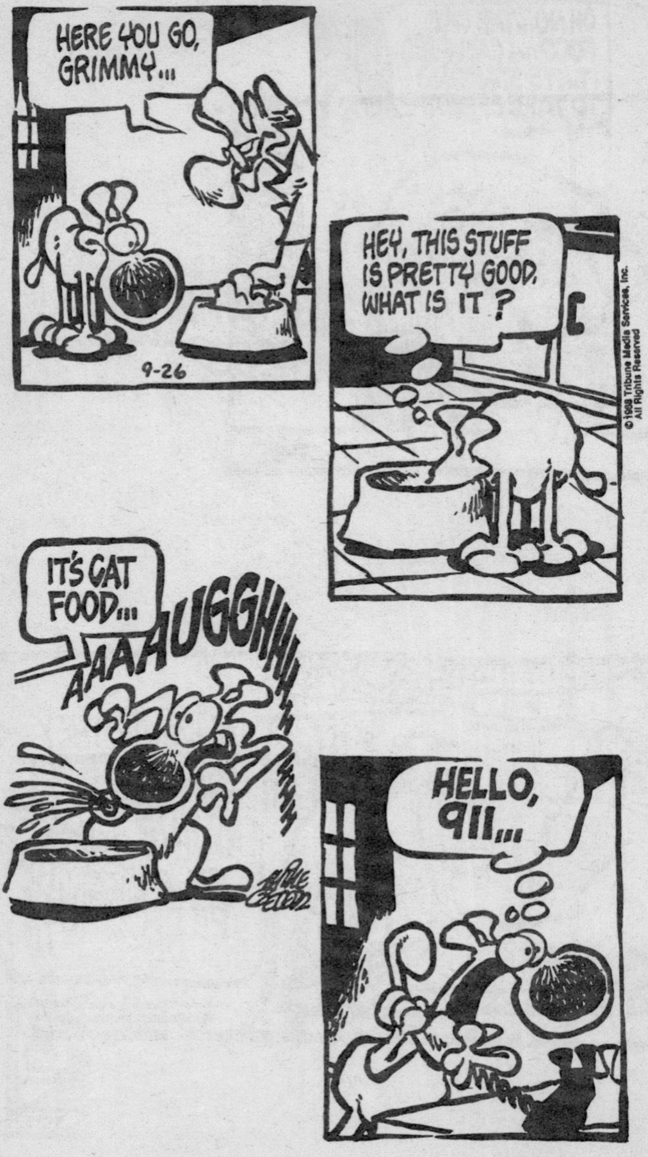
HERE YOU GO, GRIMMY...
9-26
HEY, THIS STUFF IS PRETTY GOOD. WHAT IS IT ?
© 1988 Tribune Media Services, Inc. All Rights Reserved
IT'S CAT FOOD...
AAAAUGGH
HELLO, 911...

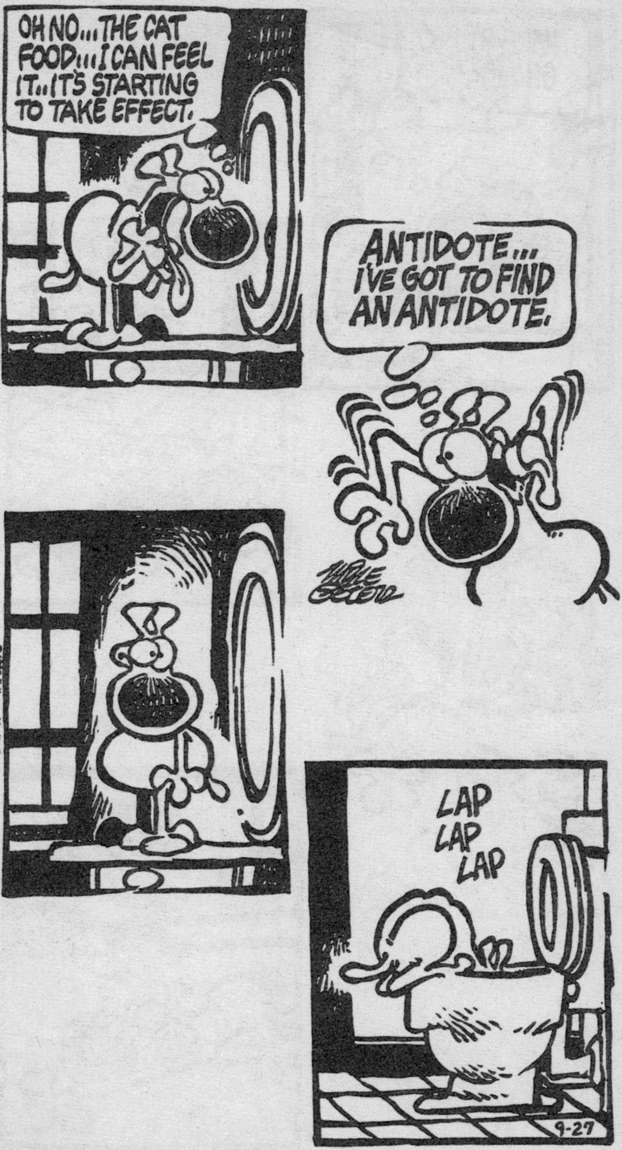
OH NO...THE CAT FOOD...I CAN FEEL IT...IT'S STARTING TO TAKE EFFECT.
ANTIDOTE... I'VE GOT TO FIND AN ANTIDOTE.
LAP LAP LAP
9-27

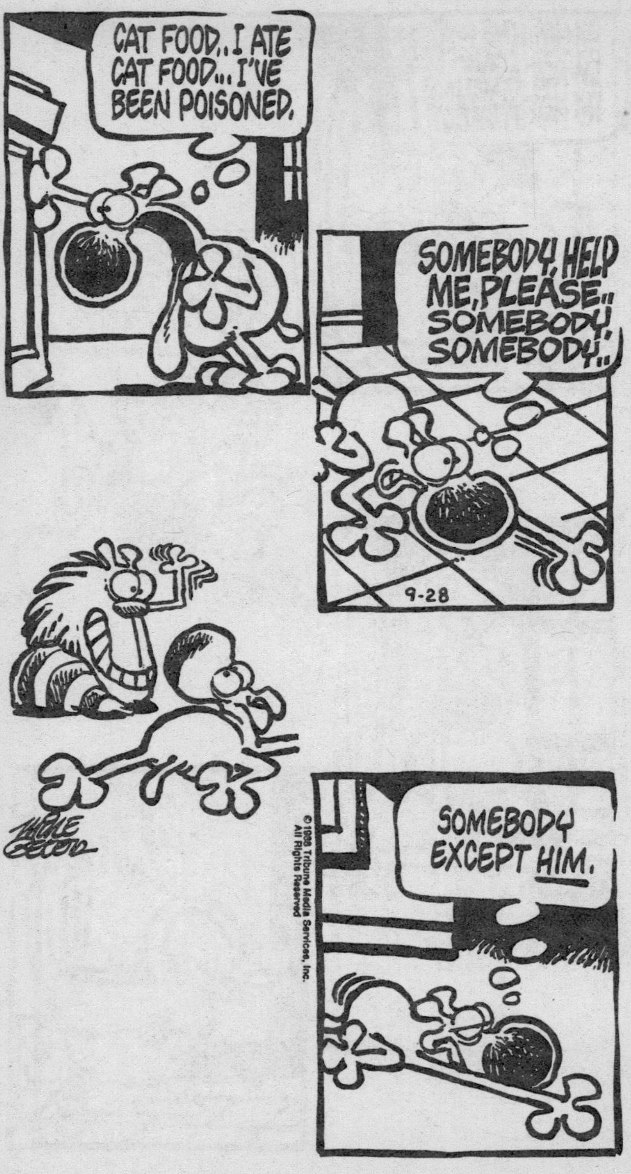
CAT FOOD.. I ATE CAT FOOD... I'VE BEEN POISONED.
SOMEBODY, HELP ME, PLEASE.. SOMEBODY, SOMEBODY..
9-28
SOMEBODY EXCEPT HIM.
© 1988 Tribune Media Services, Inc.
All Rights Reserved

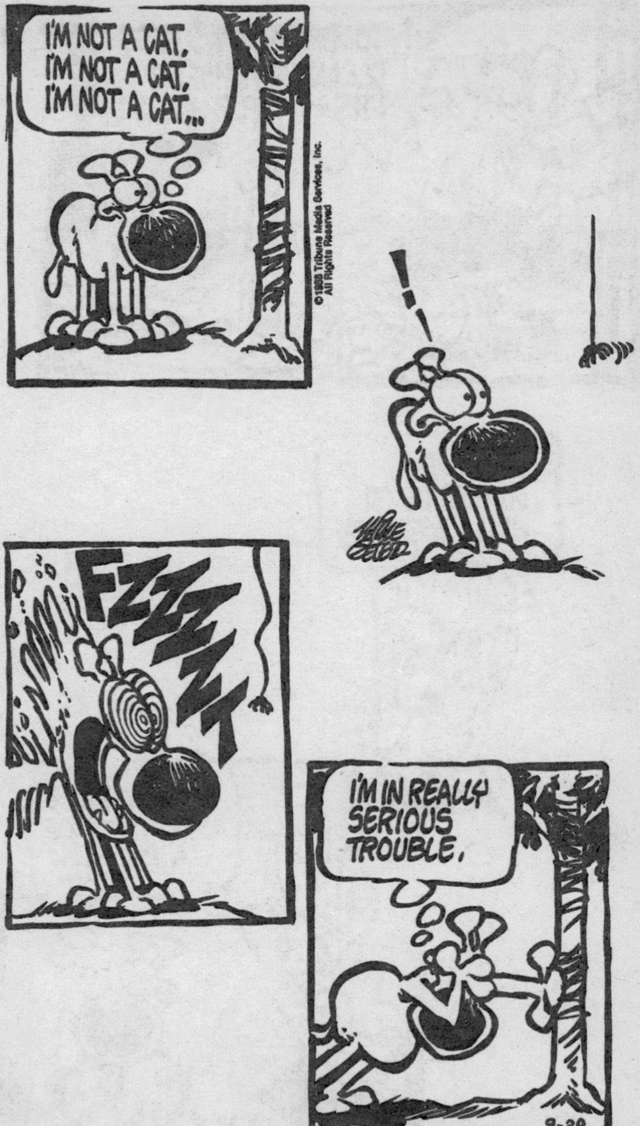
I'M NOT A CAT, I'M NOT A CAT, I'M NOT A CAT...
Tribune Media Services, Inc. All Rights Reserved
!
FZZMMT
I'M IN REALLY SERIOUS TROUBLE.
9-29

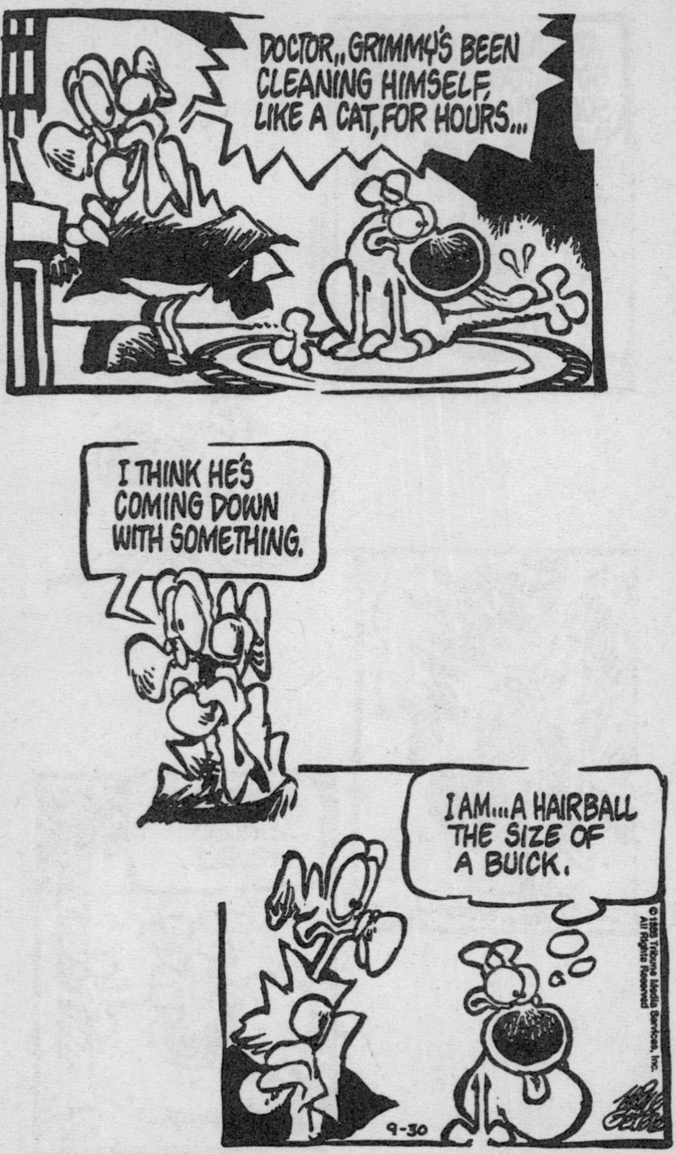
DOCTOR,, GRIMMY'S BEEN CLEANING HIMSELF, LIKE A CAT, FOR HOURS...
I THINK HE'S COMING DOWN WITH SOMETHING.
I AM...A HAIRBALL THE SIZE OF A BUICK.
9-30

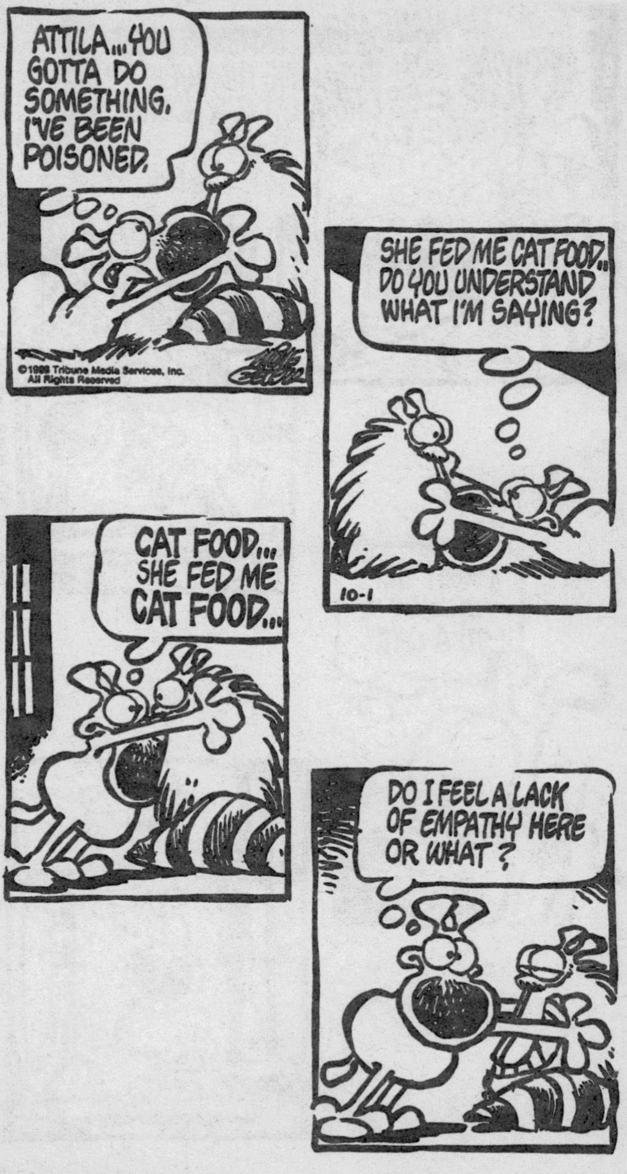
ATTILA...YOU GOTTA DO SOMETHING. I'VE BEEN POISONED.
SHE FED ME CAT FOOD... DO YOU UNDERSTAND WHAT I'M SAYING?
10-1
CAT FOOD... SHE FED ME CAT FOOD...
DO I FEEL A LACK OF EMPATHY HERE OR WHAT?

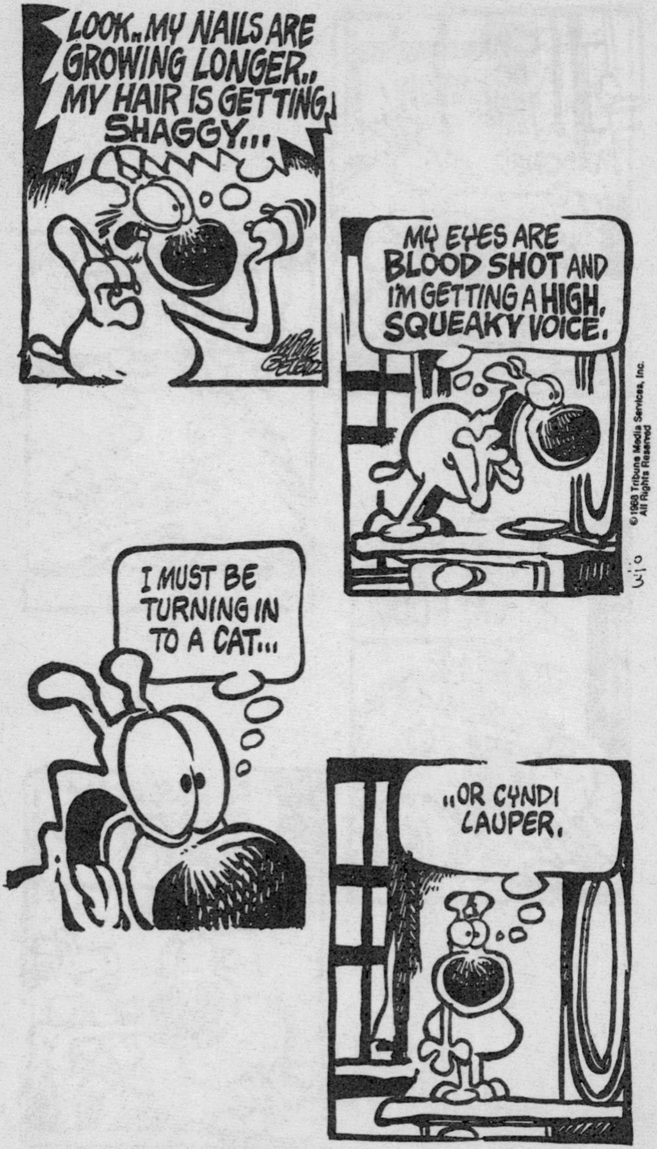
LOOK.. MY NAILS ARE GROWING LONGER.. MY HAIR IS GETTING SHAGGY...
MY EYES ARE BLOOD SHOT AND I'M GETTING A HIGH, SQUEAKY VOICE.
©1988 Tribune Media Services, Inc. All Rights Reserved
I MUST BE TURNING IN TO A CAT...
..OR CYNDI LAUPER.

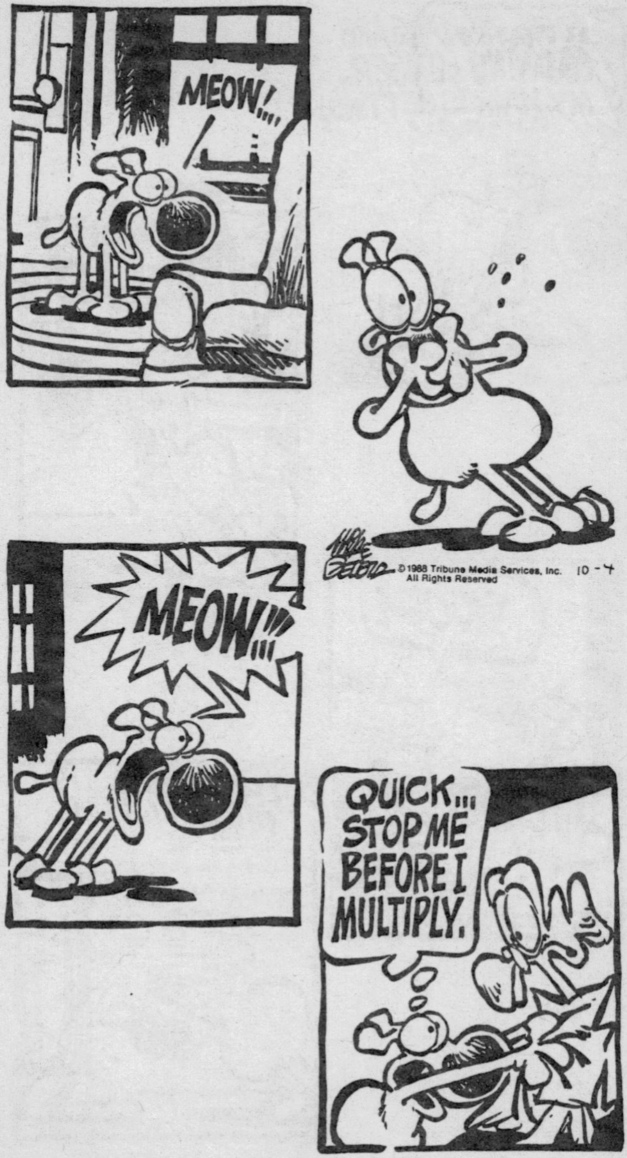
MEOW!...
MEOW!!!
QUICK... STOP ME BEFORE I MULTIPLY.
©1988 Tribune Media Services, Inc. All Rights Reserved
10-4

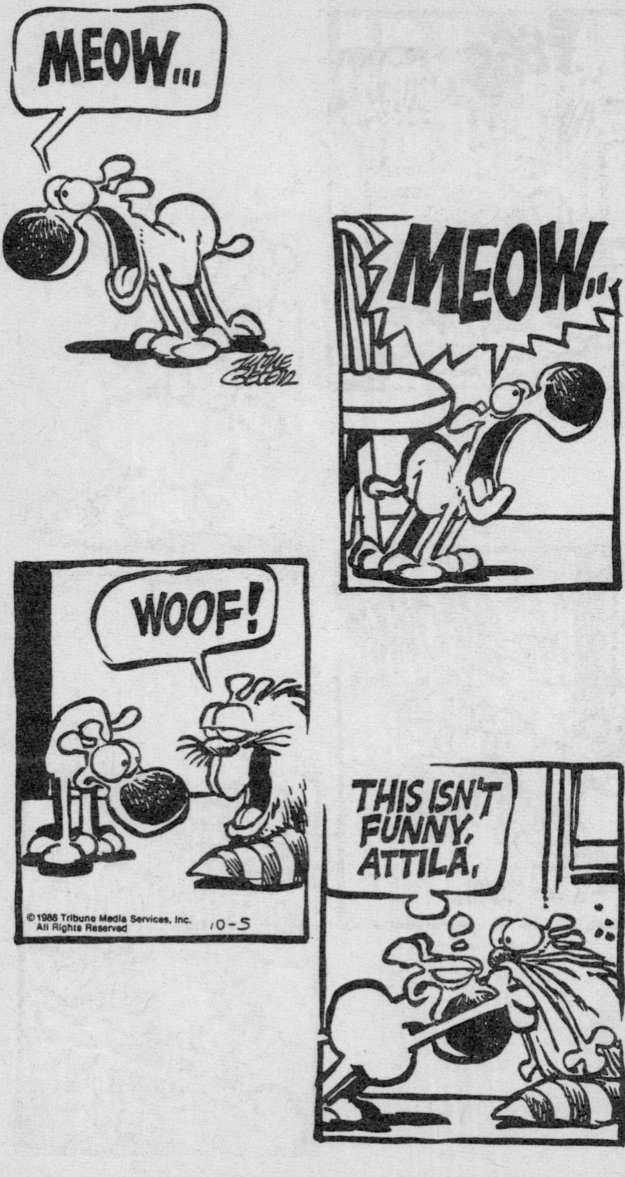
MEOW...
MEOW...
WOOF!
THIS ISN'T FUNNY, ATTILA.

10-5

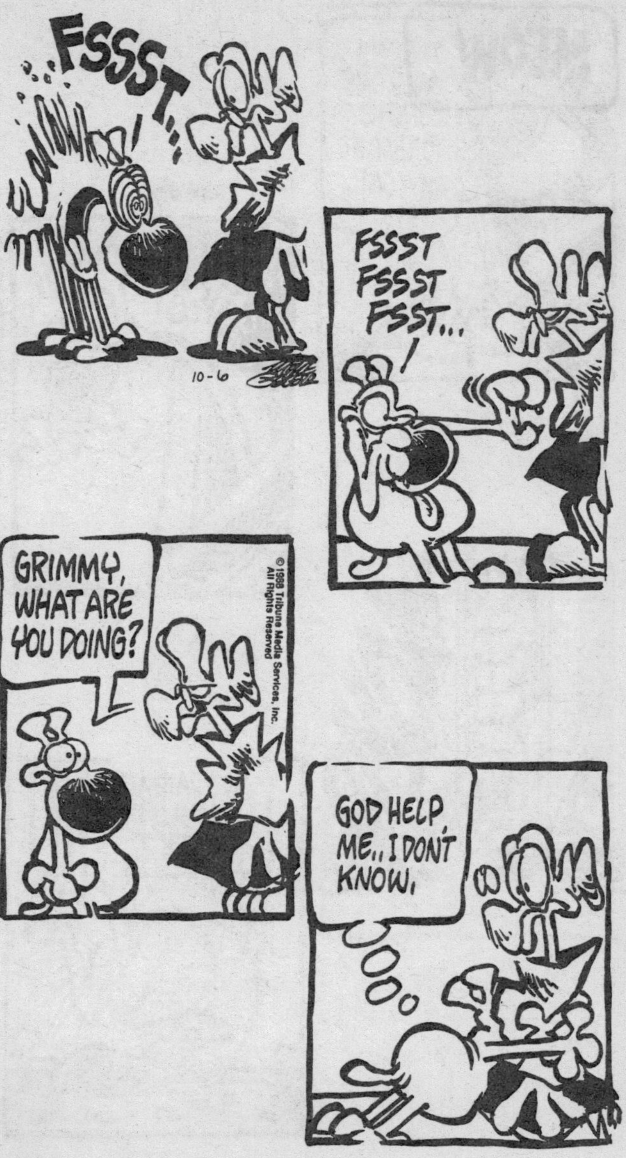
..FSSST...!
10-6
FSSST
FSSST
FSST...!
GRIMMY, WHAT ARE YOU DOING?
© 1988 Tribune Media Services, Inc.
All Rights Reserved
GOD HELP ME.. I DON'T KNOW.

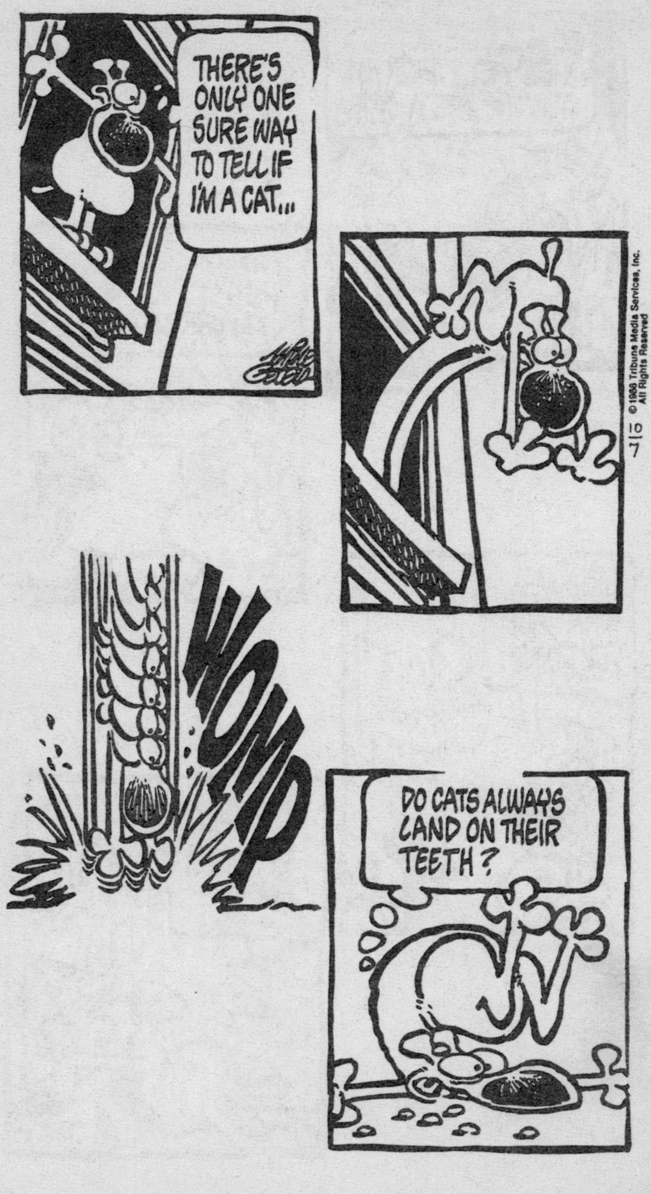
THERE'S ONLY ONE SURE WAY TO TELL IF I'M A CAT...
WOMP
DO CATS ALWAYS LAND ON THEIR TEETH?
© 1986 Tribune Media Services, Inc. All Rights Reserved

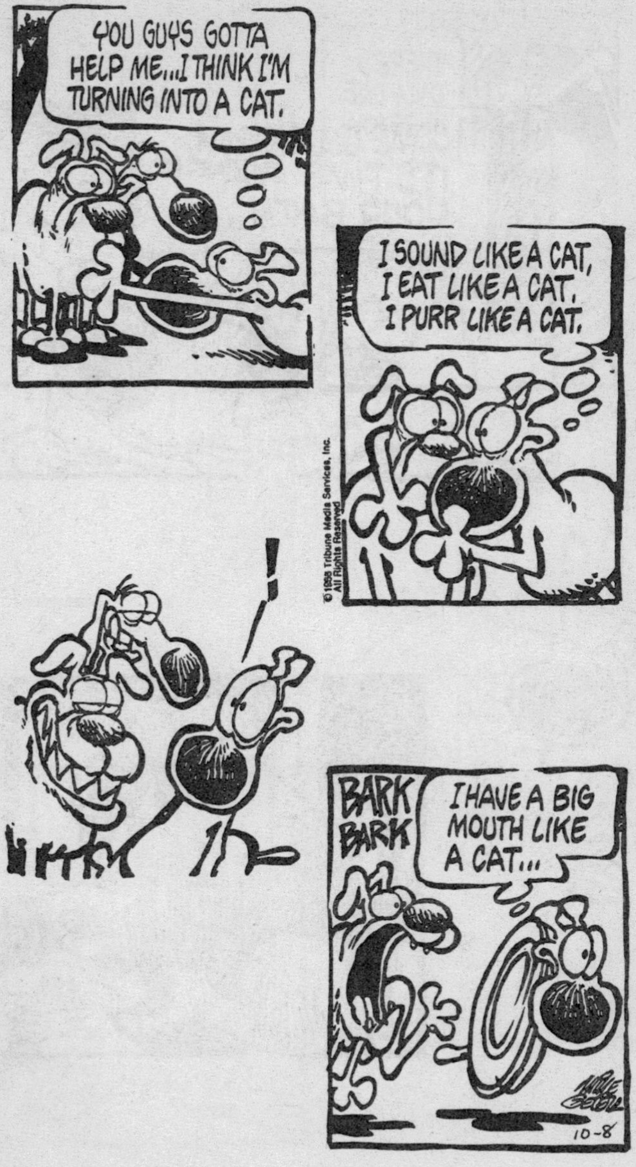
YOU GUYS GOTTA HELP ME...I THINK I'M TURNING INTO A CAT.
I SOUND LIKE A CAT, I EAT LIKE A CAT, I PURR LIKE A CAT.
© 1988 Tribune Media Services, Inc. All Rights Reserved
!
BARK BARK
I HAVE A BIG MOUTH LIKE A CAT...
10-8

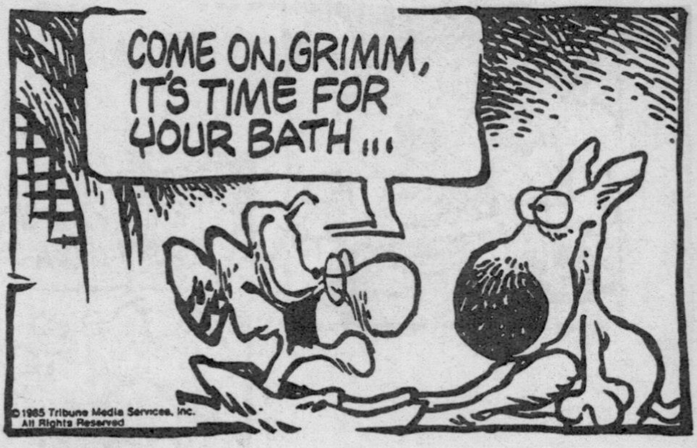
COME ON, GRIMM, IT'S TIME FOR YOUR BATH...
©1985 Tribune Media Services, Inc.
All Rights Reserved

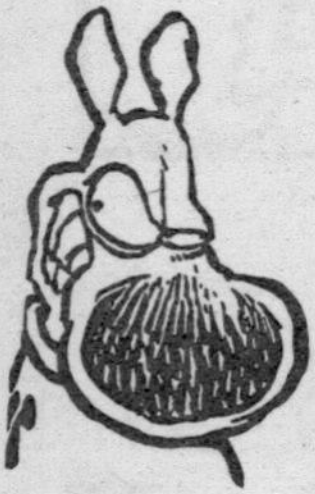

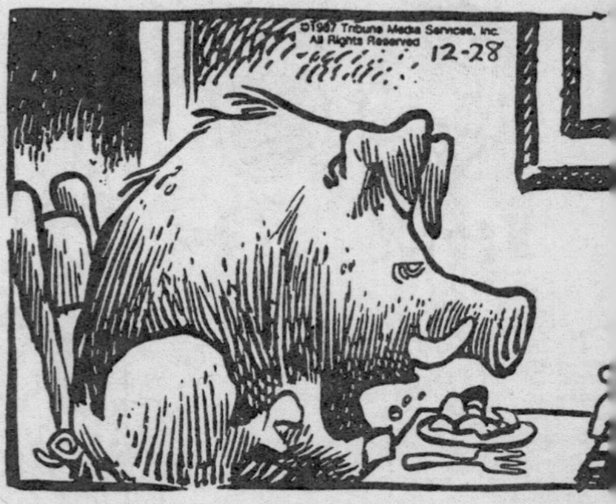
©1987 Tribune Media Services, Inc.
All Rights Reserved
12-28

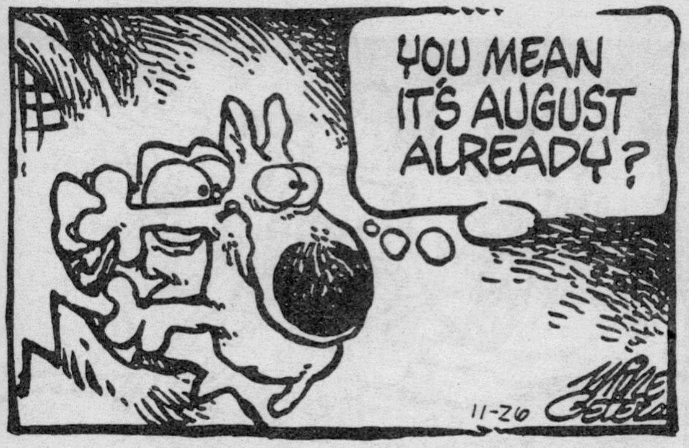
YOU MEAN IT'S AUGUST ALREADY?
11-26
MIKE PETERS

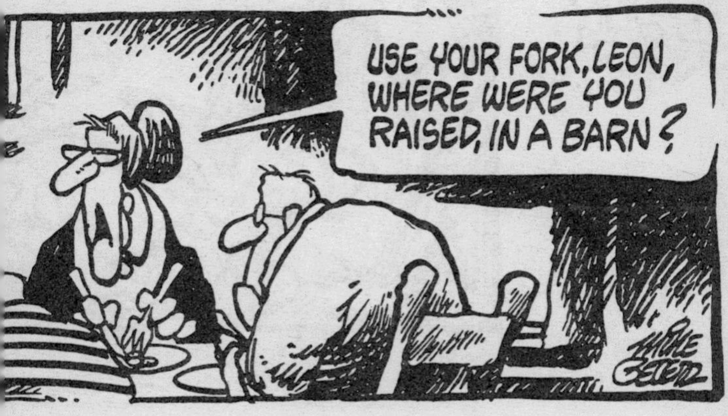
USE YOUR FORK, LEON, WHERE WERE YOU RAISED, IN A BARN?
MIKE PETERS

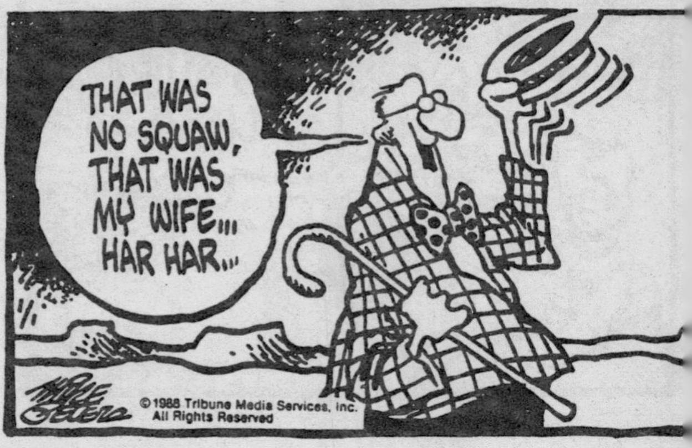
THAT WAS NO SQUAW, THAT WAS MY WIFE... HAR HAR...
©1988 Tribune Media Services, Inc. All Rights Reserved

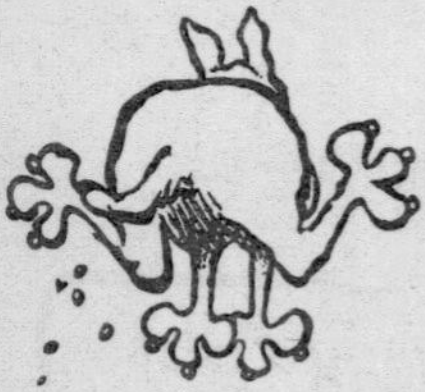

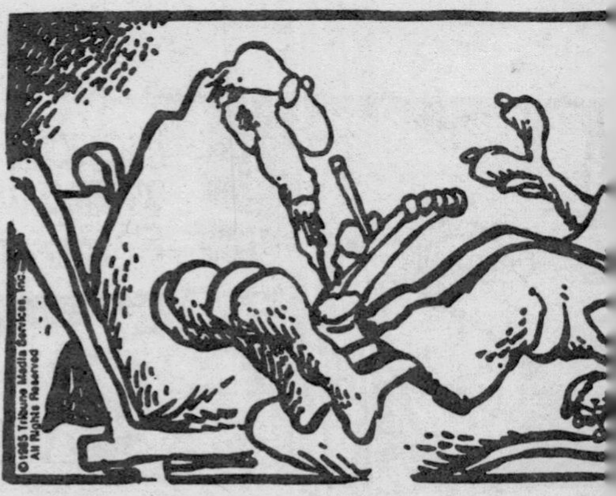

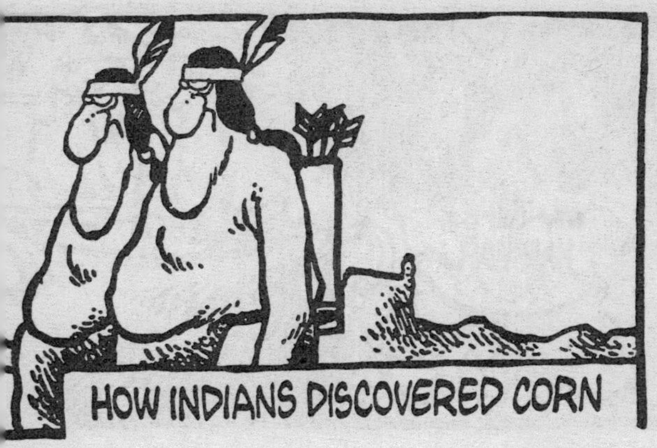
HOW INDIANS DISCOVERED CORN

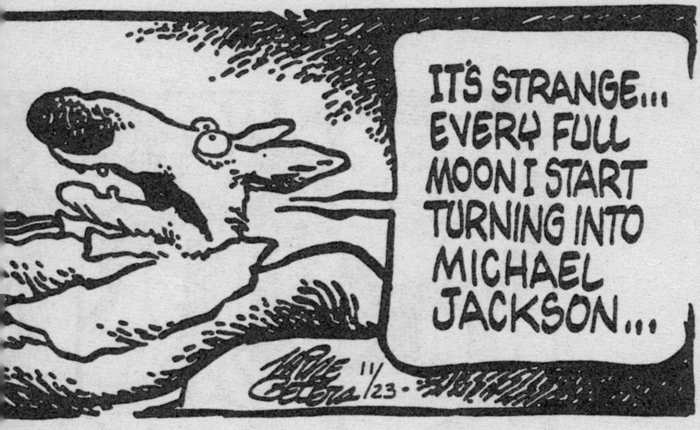
IT'S STRANGE...
EVERY FULL MOON I START TURNING INTO MICHAEL JACKSON...

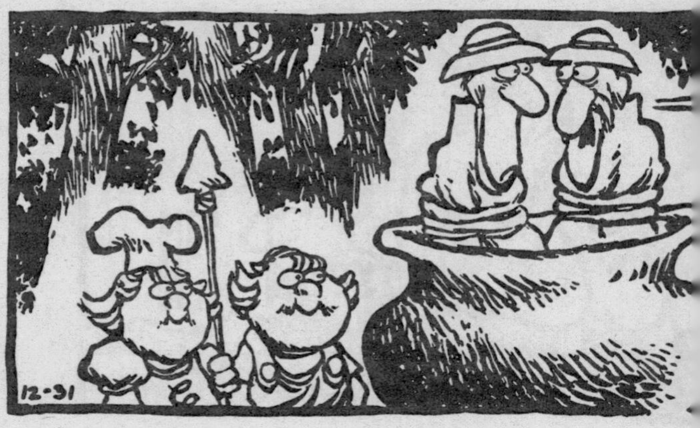
12-31

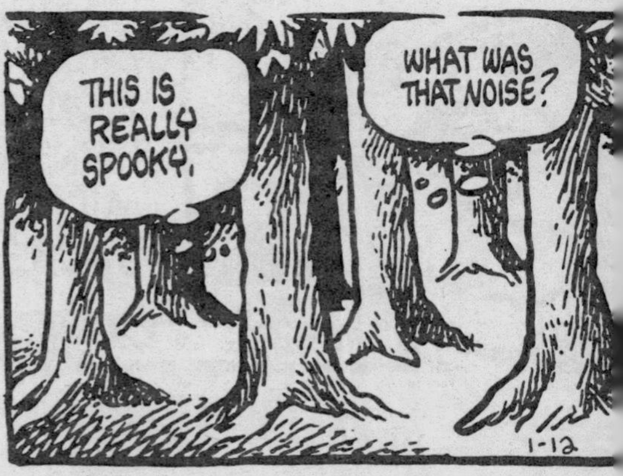
THIS IS REALLY SPOOKY.
WHAT WAS THAT NOISE?
1-12

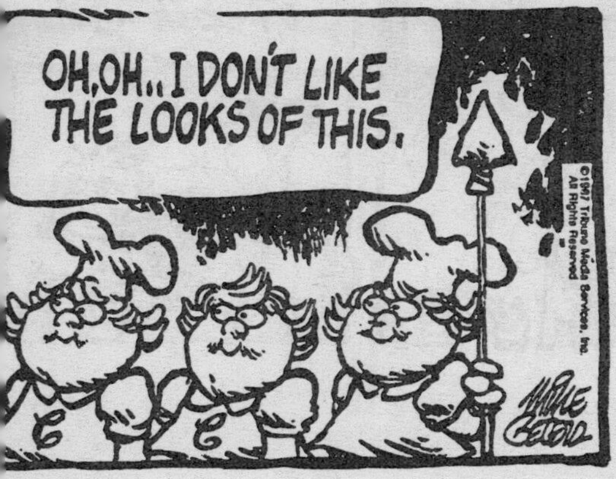

OH,OH.. I DON'T LIKE THE LOOKS OF THIS.
©1987 Tribune Media Services, Inc. All Rights Reserved

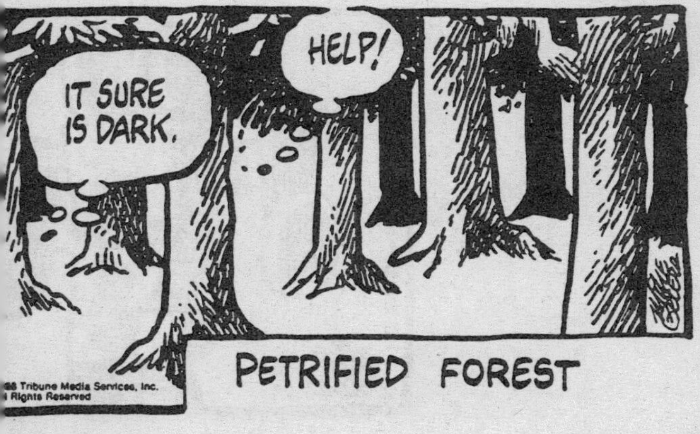

IT SURE IS DARK.
HELP!
PETRIFIED FOREST
Tribune Media Services, Inc.
Rights Reserved

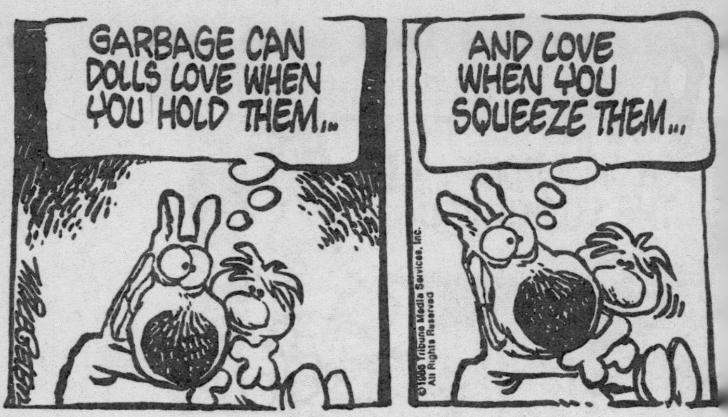
GARBAGE CAN DOLLS LOVE WHEN YOU HOLD THEM...
AND LOVE WHEN YOU SQUEEZE THEM...
©1988 Tribune Media Services, Inc. All Rights Reserved

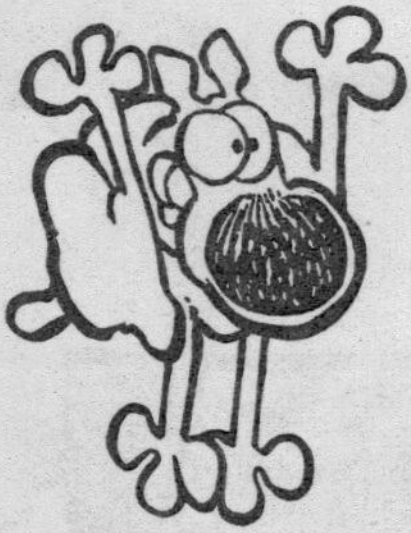

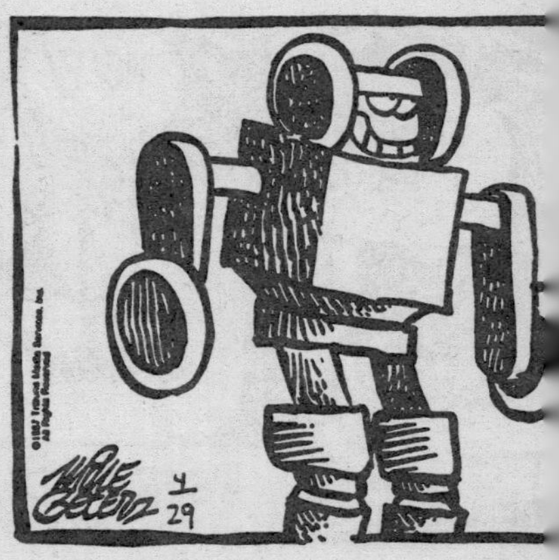
4
29

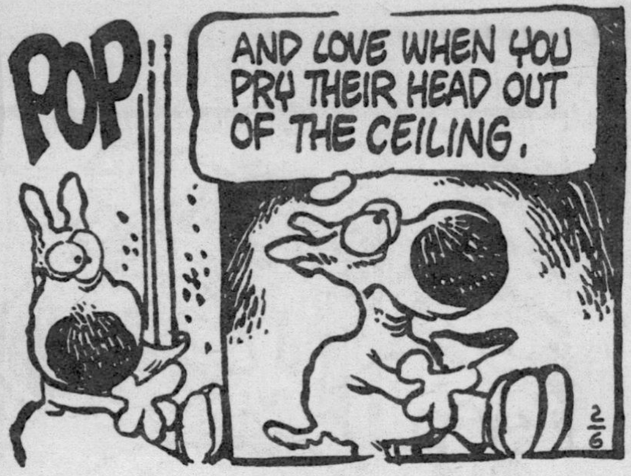
POP!
AND LOVE WHEN YOU PRY THEIR HEAD OUT OF THE CEILING.
2/6

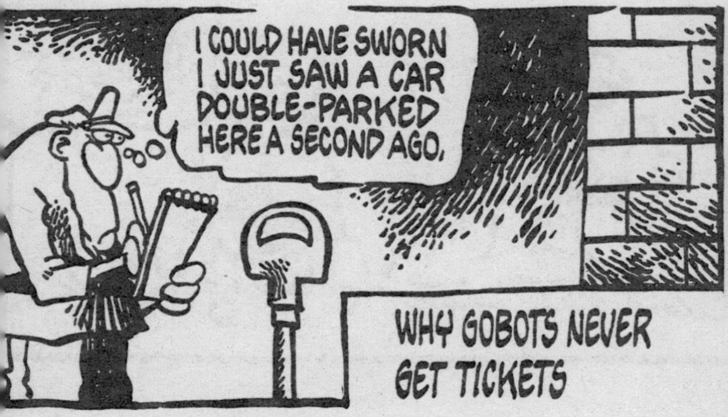
I COULD HAVE SWORN I JUST SAW A CAR DOUBLE-PARKED HERE A SECOND AGO.
WHY GOBOTS NEVER GET TICKETS

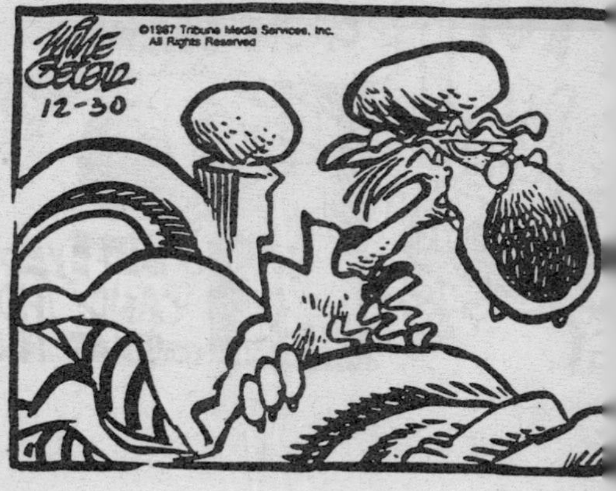
©1987 Tribune Media Services, Inc.
All Rights Reserved
12-30

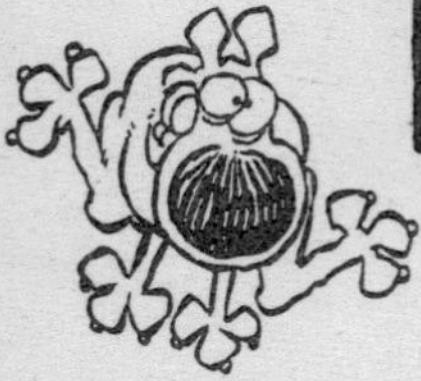

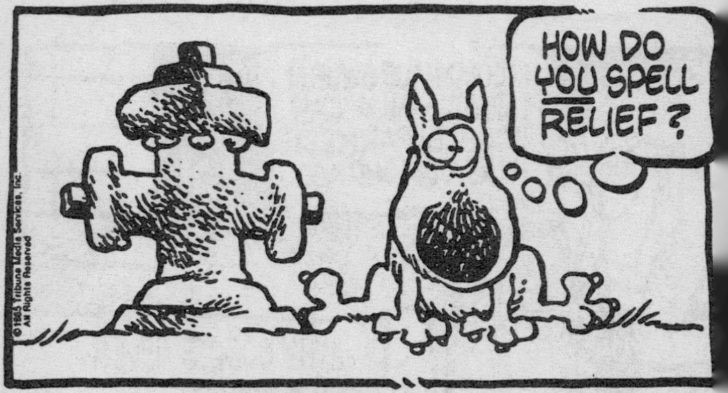
HOW DO YOU SPELL RELIEF?
Tribune Media Services, Inc.
All Rights Reserved

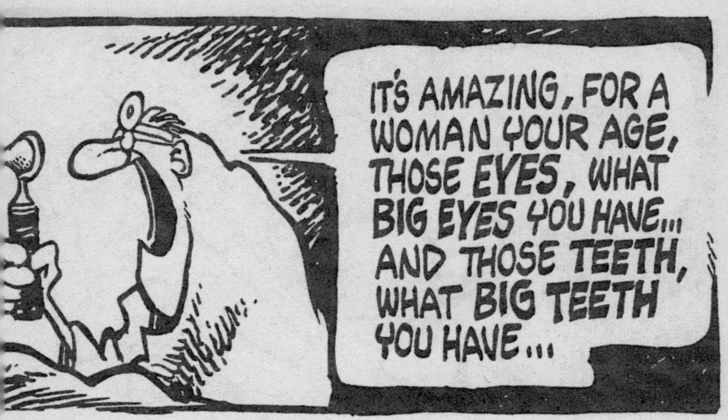
IT'S AMAZING, FOR A WOMAN YOUR AGE, THOSE EYES, WHAT BIG EYES YOU HAVE... AND THOSE TEETH, WHAT BIG TEETH YOU HAVE...

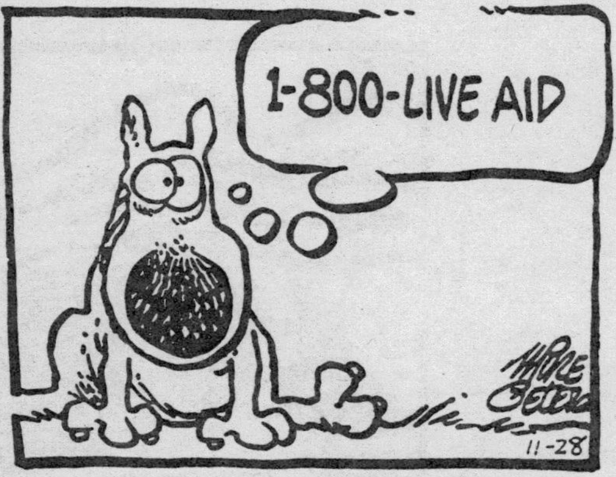
1-800-LIVE AID
11-28

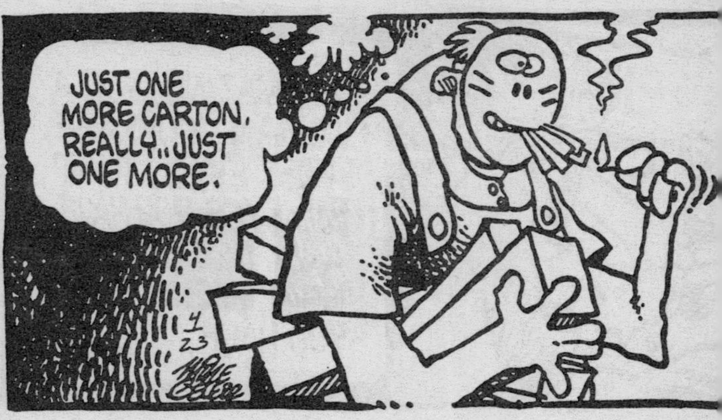
JUST ONE MORE CARTON. REALLY.. JUST ONE MORE.
4
23

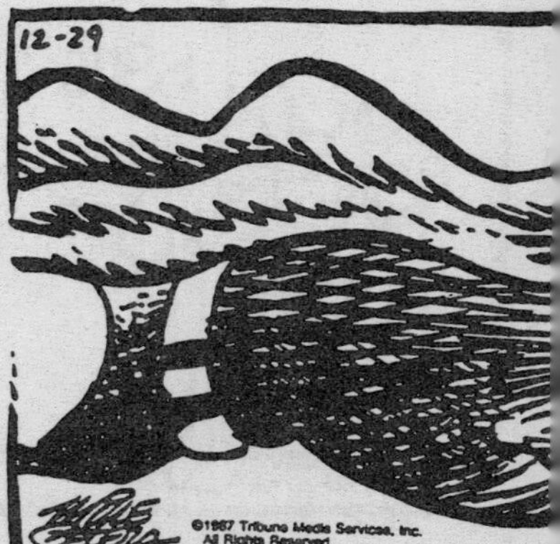
12-29
©1987 Tribune Media Services, Inc.
All Rights Reserved

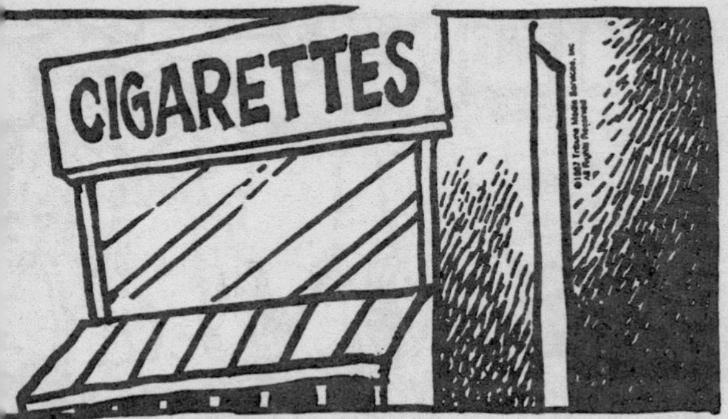
CIGARETTES

TEXAS CHAIN SMOKING MASSACRE

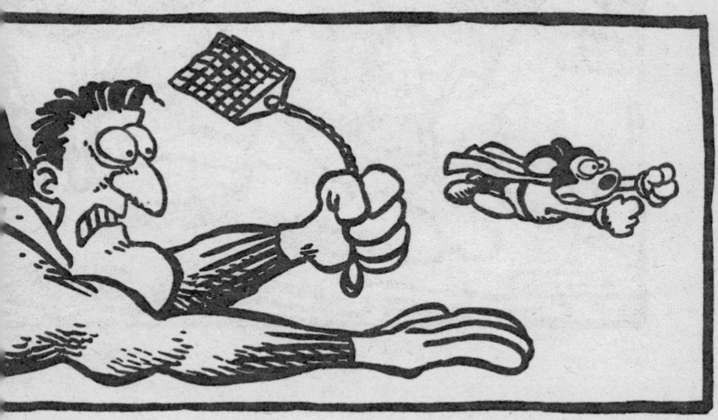

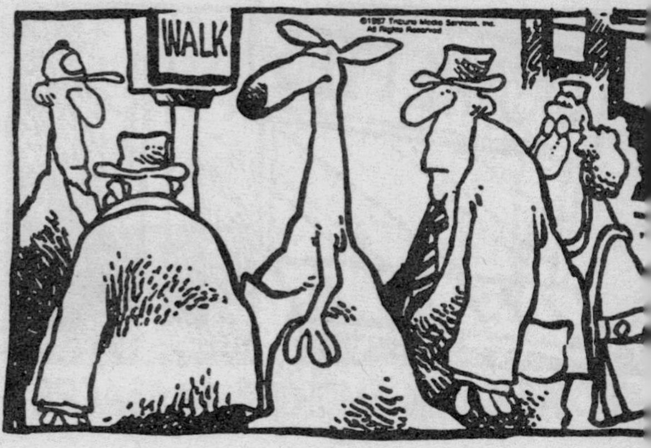
WALK
©1987 Tribune Media Services, Inc.
All Rights Reserved

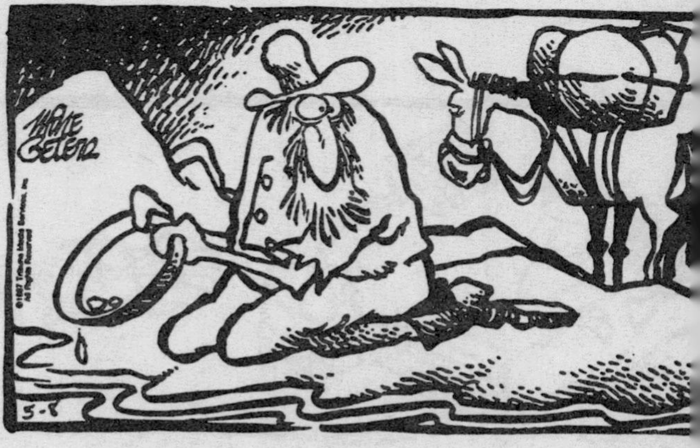
©1987 Tribune Media Services, Inc
All Rights Reserved
5-8

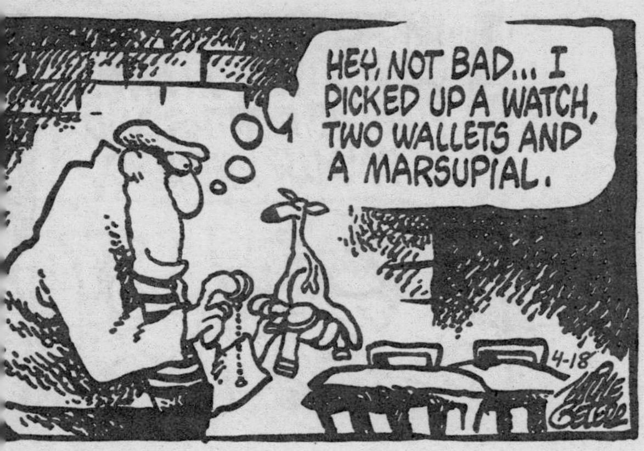
HEY, NOT BAD... I PICKED UP A WATCH, TWO WALLETS AND A MARSUPIAL.
4-18

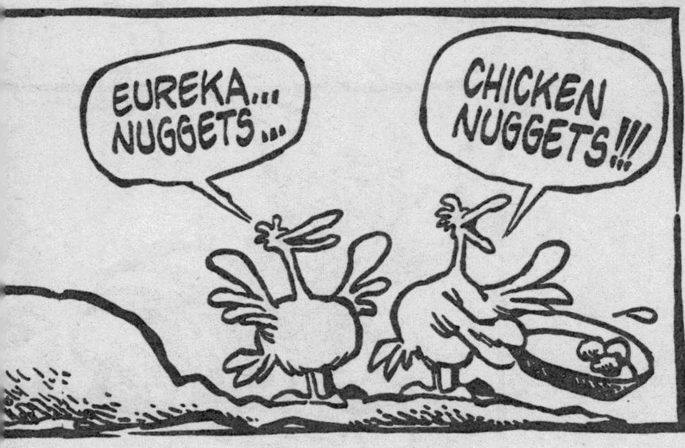
EUREKA... NUGGETS...
CHICKEN NUGGETS!!!

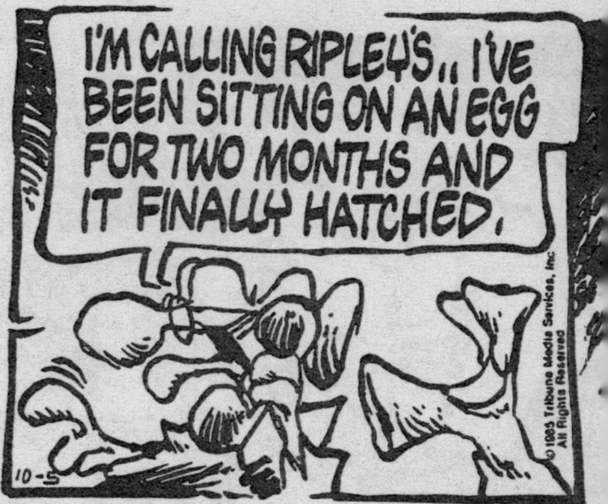
I'M CALLING RIPLEY'S.. I'VE BEEN SITTING ON AN EGG FOR TWO MONTHS AND IT FINALLY HATCHED.
© 1985 Tribune Media Services, Inc
All Rights Reserved
10-5

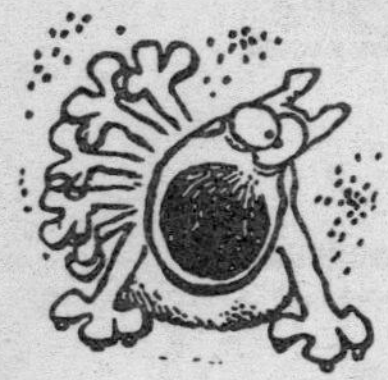

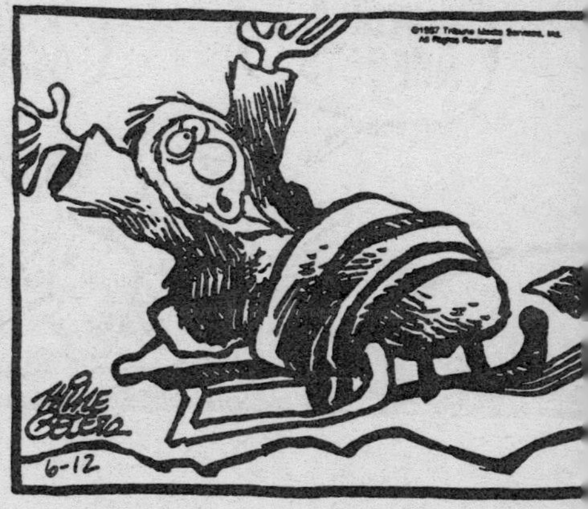
6-12

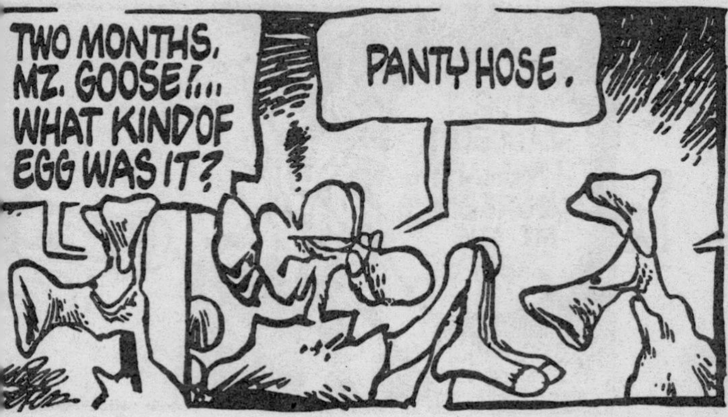
TWO MONTHS, MZ. GOOSE!... WHAT KIND OF EGG WAS IT?
PANTY HOSE.

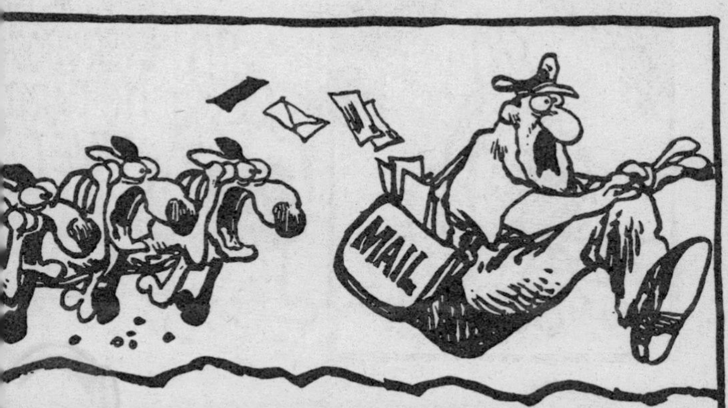
MAIL

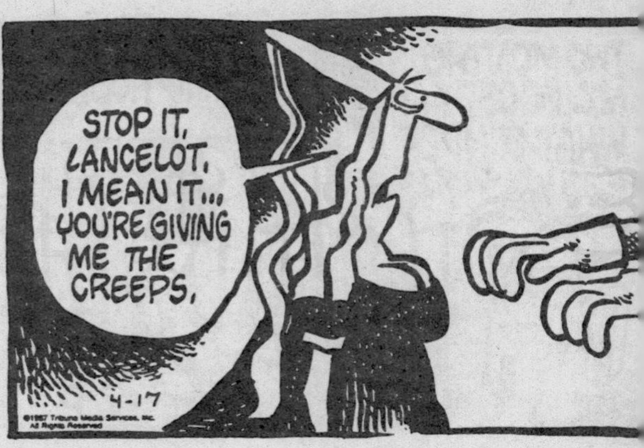
STOP IT, LANCELOT. I MEAN IT... YOU'RE GIVING ME THE CREEPS.
4-17
©1987 Tribune Media Services, Inc. All Rights Reserved

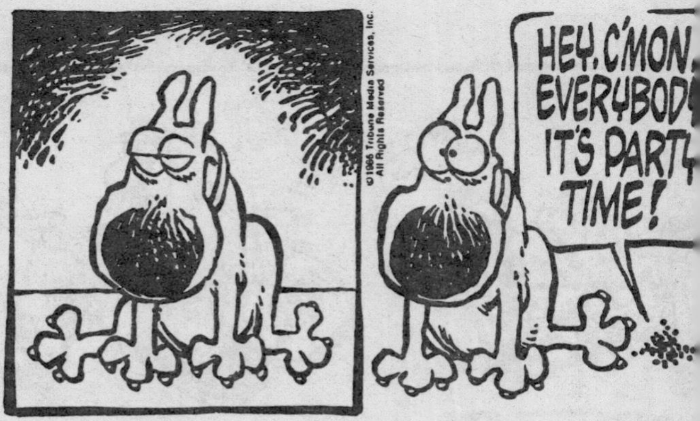
©1986 Tribune Media Services, Inc. All Rights Reserved
HEY, C'MON, EVERYBOD IT'S PARTY TIME!

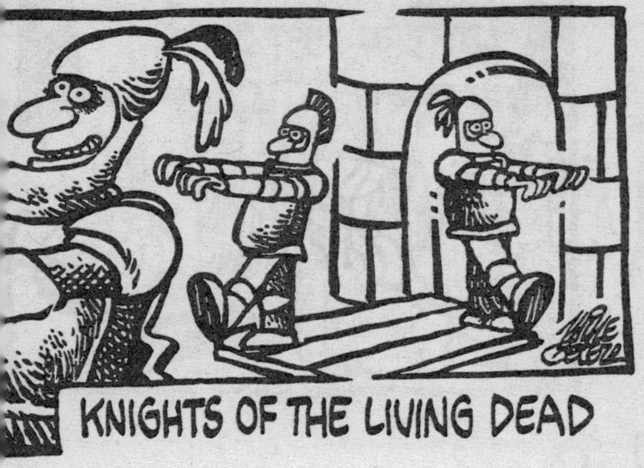

KNIGHTS OF THE LIVING DEAD

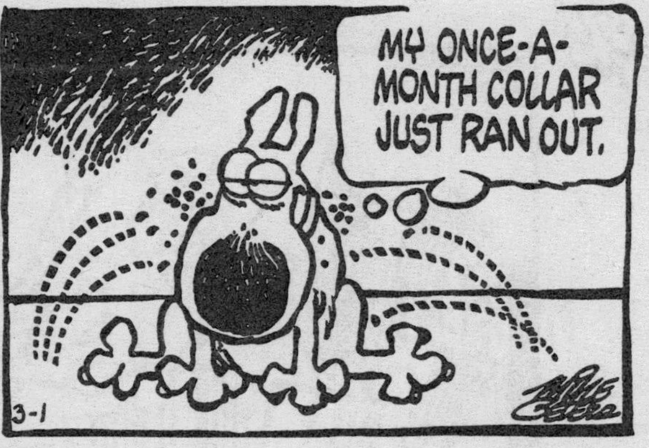

MY ONCE-A-MONTH COLLAR JUST RAN OUT.
3-1

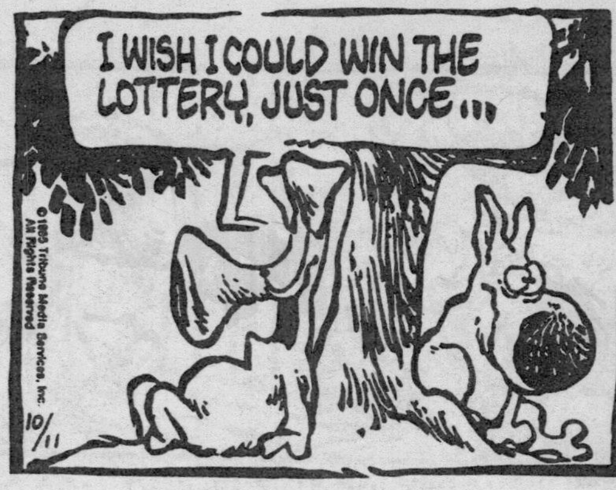
I WISH I COULD WIN THE LOTTERY, JUST ONCE...
Tribune Media Services, Inc.
All Rights Reserved
10/11

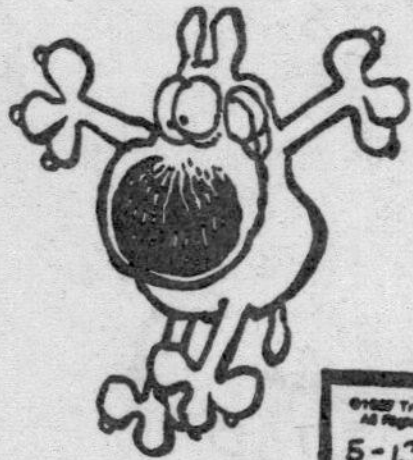

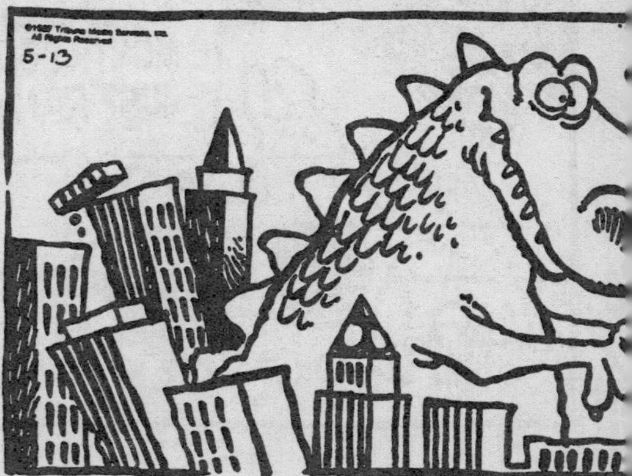
5-13

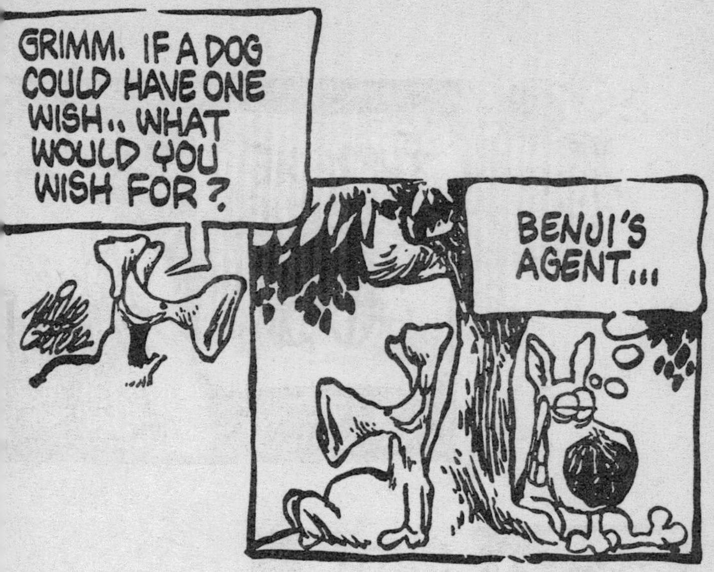
GRIMM. IF A DOG COULD HAVE ONE WISH.. WHAT WOULD YOU WISH FOR?
BENJI'S AGENT...

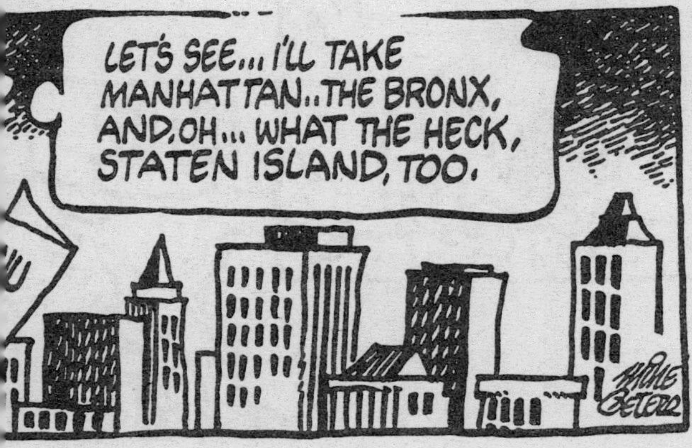
LET'S SEE... I'LL TAKE MANHATTAN..THE BRONX, AND,OH... WHAT THE HECK, STATEN ISLAND, TOO.

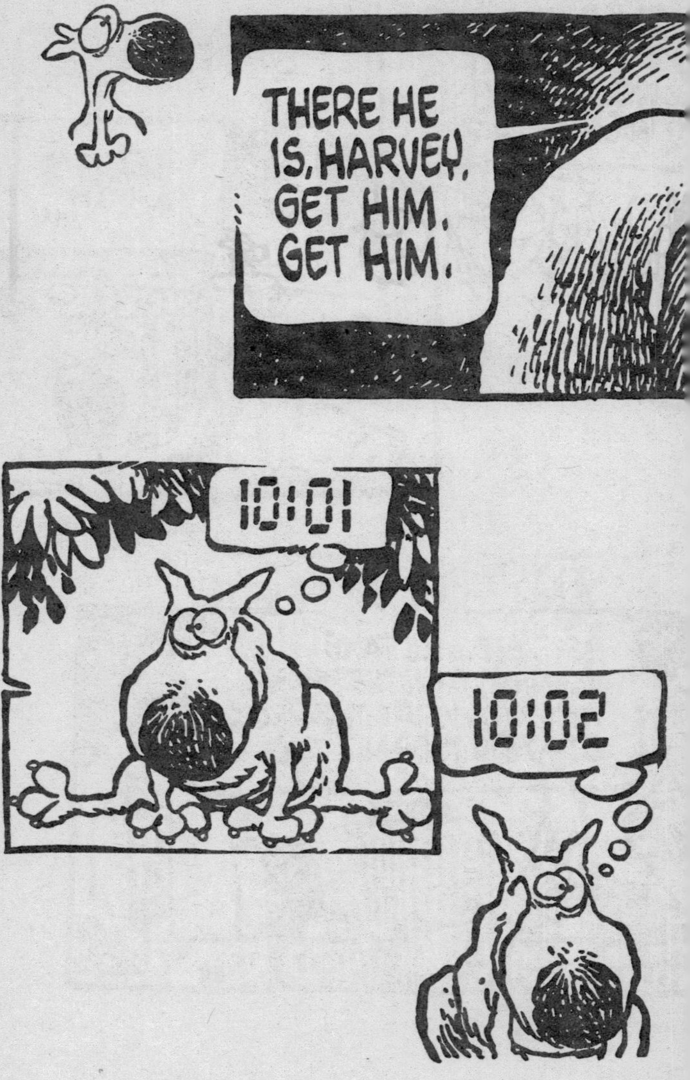
THERE HE IS, HARVEY. GET HIM. GET HIM.
10:01
10:02

THE
BUTTON

5/28

I'M A DIGITAL
WATCH DOG.

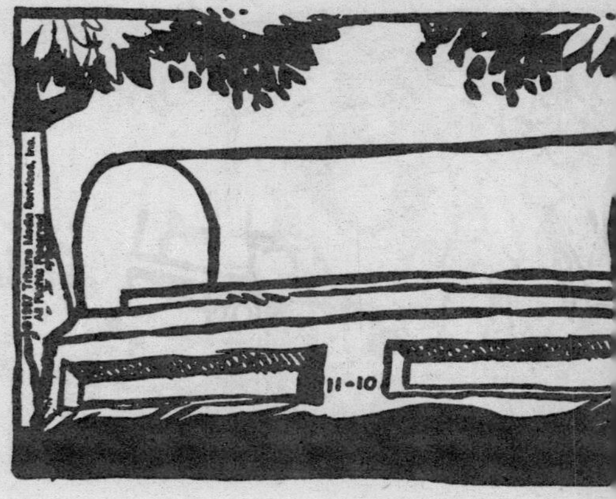
©1987 Tribune Media Services, Inc.
All Rights Reserved
11-10

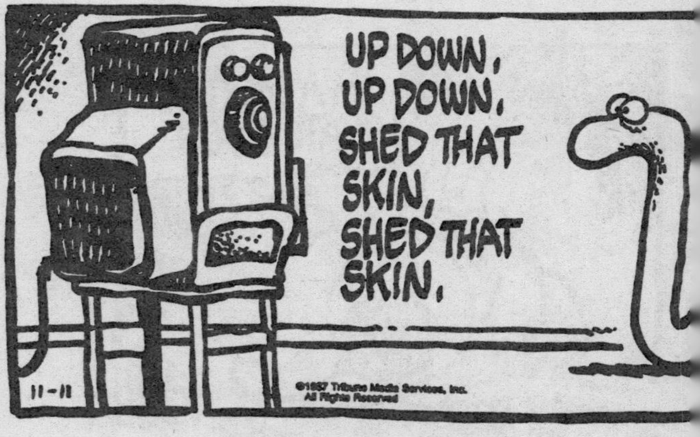
UP DOWN,
UP DOWN,
SHED THAT
SKIN,
SHED THAT
SKIN.
11-11
©1987 Tribune Media Services, Inc.
All Rights Reserved

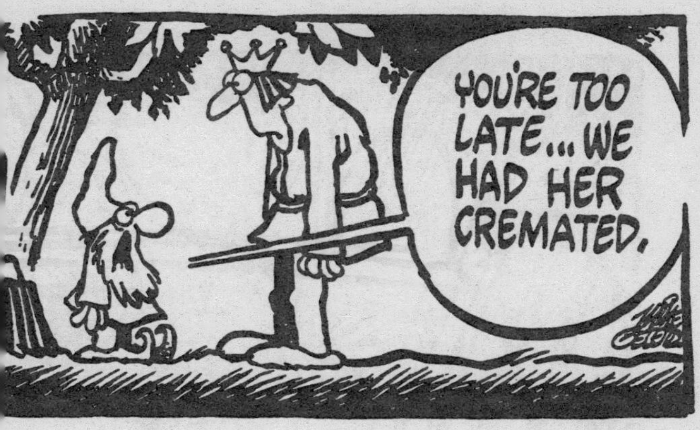
YOU'RE TOO LATE... WE HAD HER CREMATED.

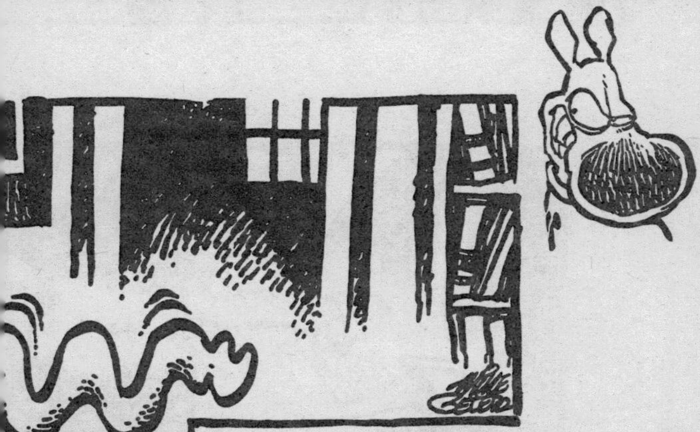

REPTILE AEROBICS

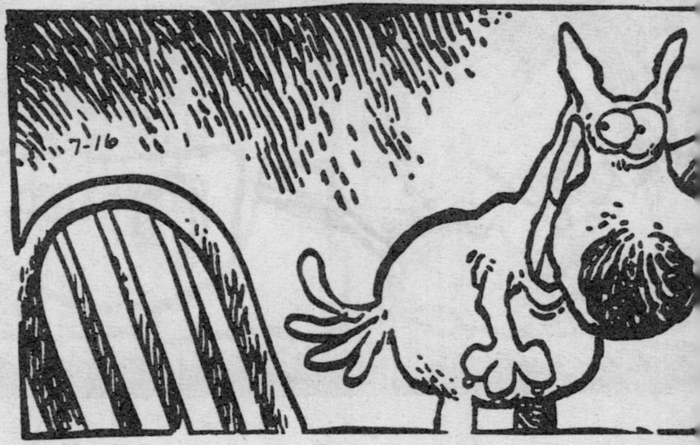
7-16

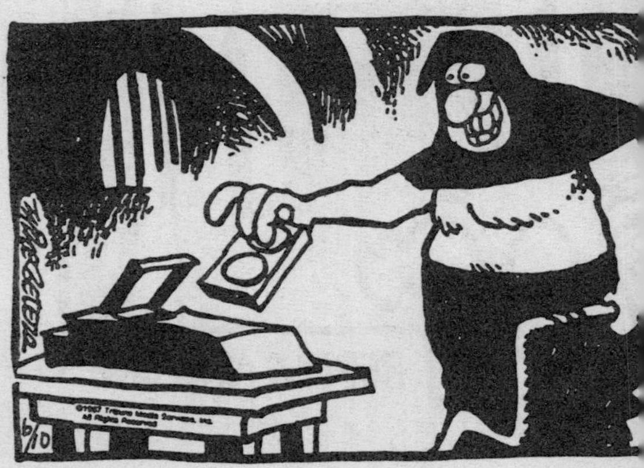
6/10

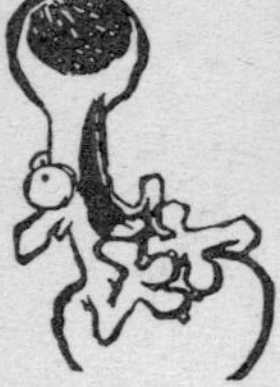

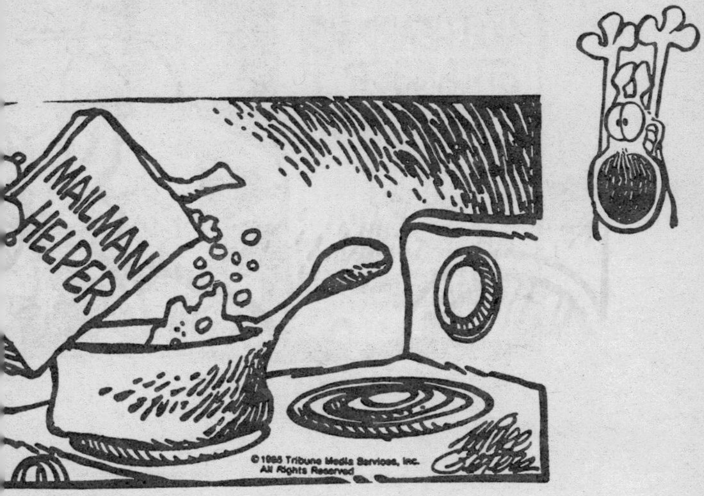
MAILMAN HELPER
© 1985 Tribune Media Services, Inc.
All Rights Reserved

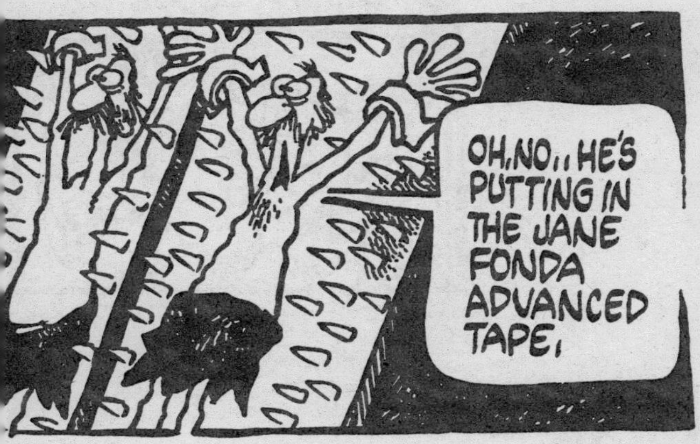
OH, NO.. HE'S PUTTING IN THE JANE FONDA ADVANCED TAPE.

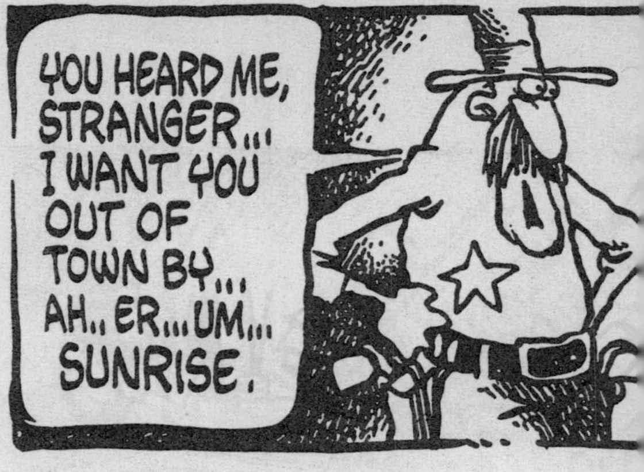
YOU HEARD ME, STRANGER... I WANT YOU OUT OF TOWN BY... AH.. ER... UM... SUNRISE.

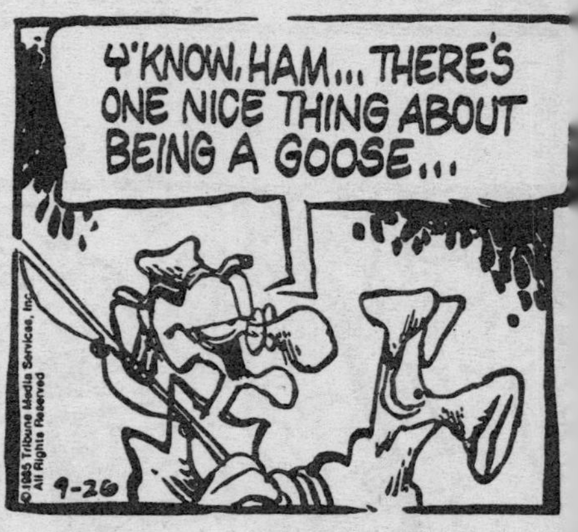
Y'KNOW, HAM... THERE'S ONE NICE THING ABOUT BEING A GOOSE...
©1985 Tribune Media Services, Inc. All Rights Reserved
9-26

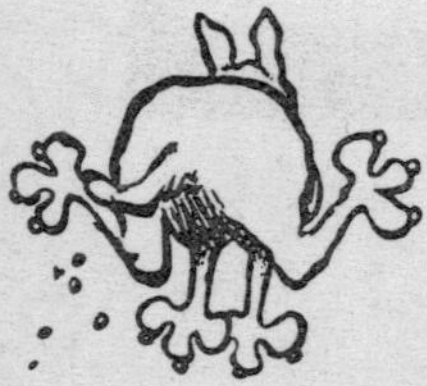

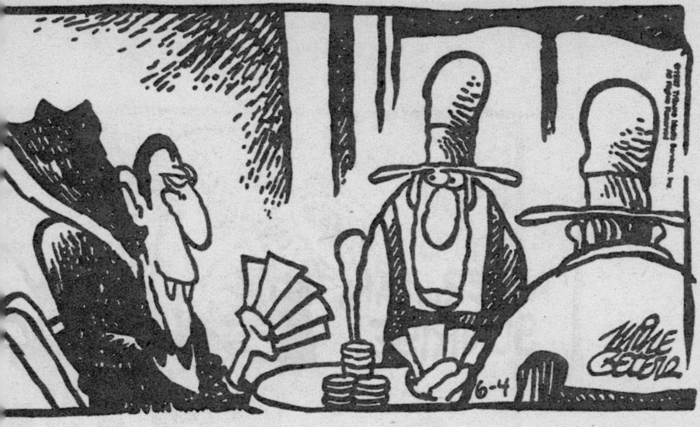
6-4

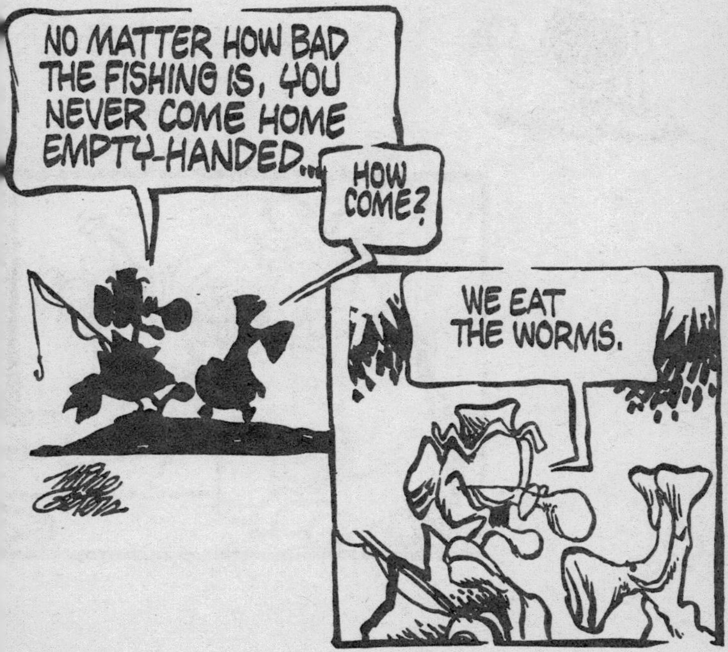
NO MATTER HOW BAD THE FISHING IS, YOU NEVER COME HOME EMPTY-HANDED...
HOW COME?
WE EAT THE WORMS.

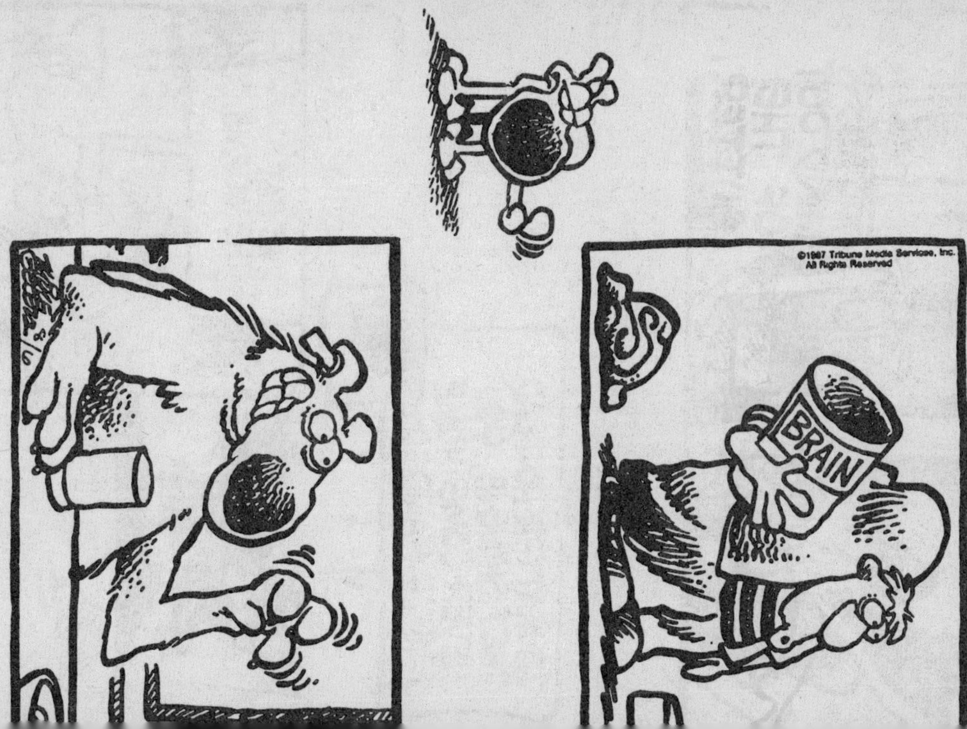
BRAIN

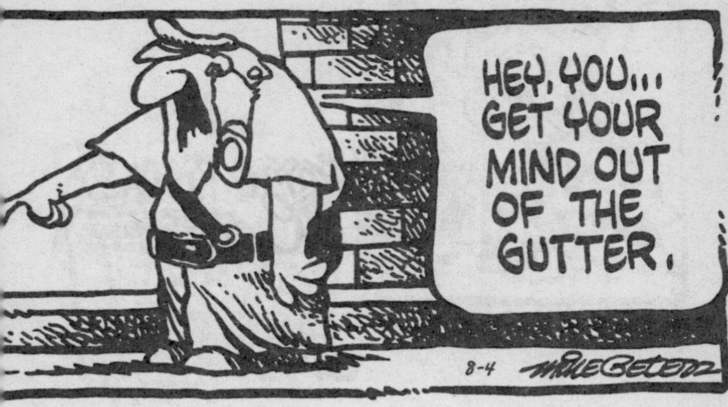
HEY, YOU... GET YOUR MIND OUT OF THE GUTTER.
8-4

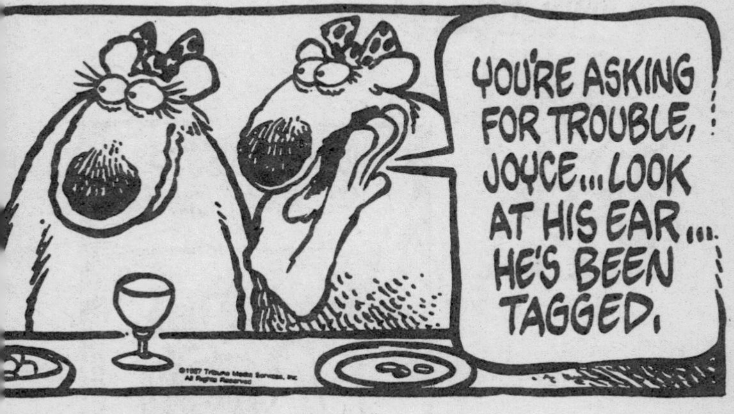
YOU'RE ASKING FOR TROUBLE, JOYCE... LOOK AT HIS EAR... HE'S BEEN TAGGED.

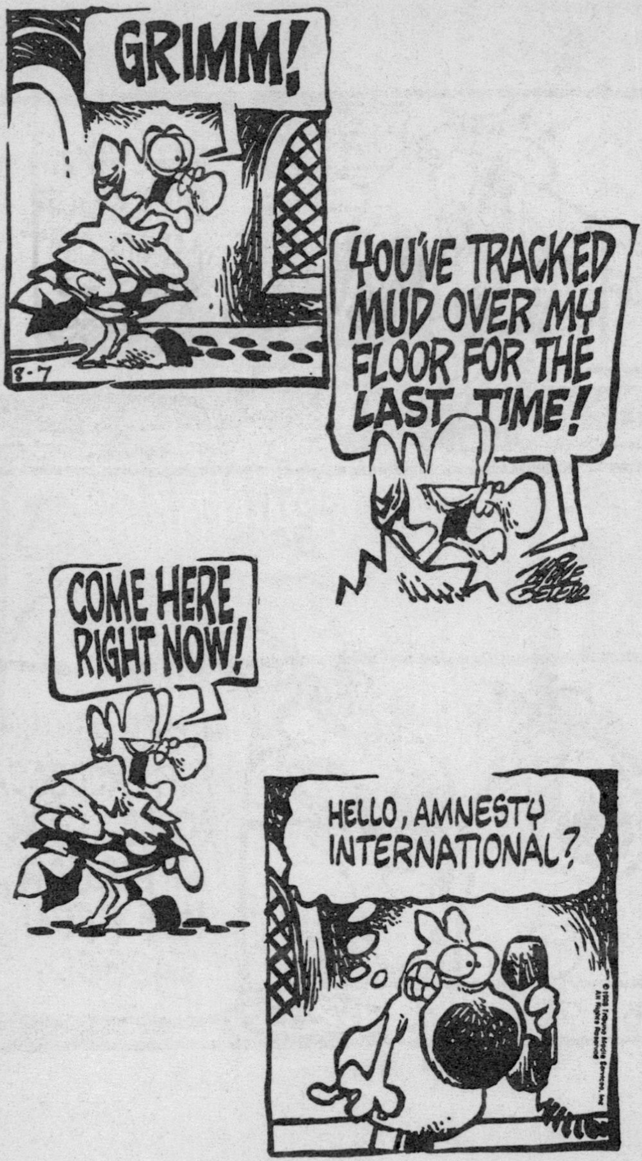
GRIMM!
8-7
YOU'VE TRACKED MUD OVER MY FLOOR FOR THE LAST TIME!
COME HERE RIGHT NOW!
HELLO, AMNESTY INTERNATIONAL?

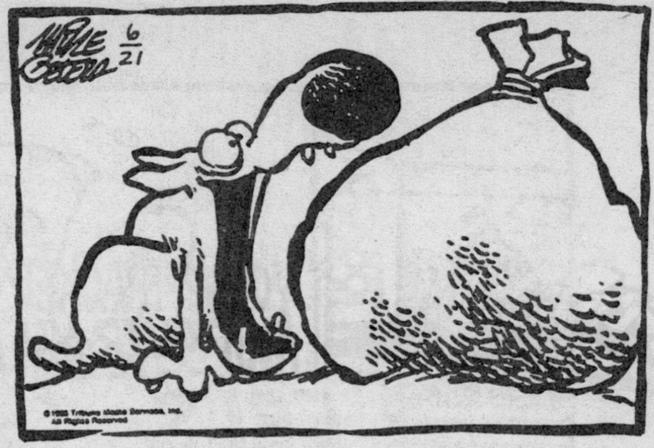

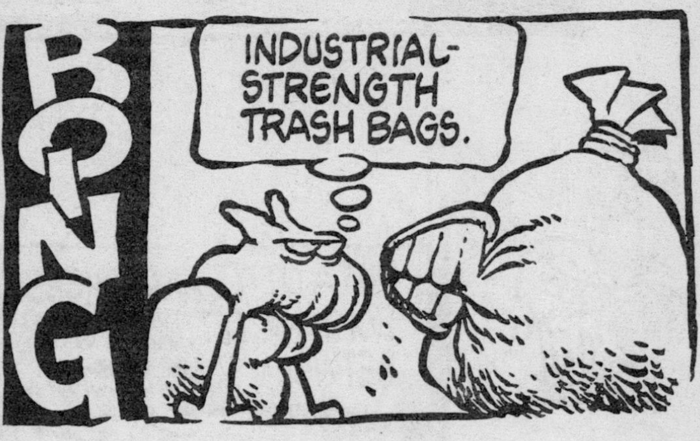
BONG
INDUSTRIAL-
STRENGTH
TRASH BAGS.

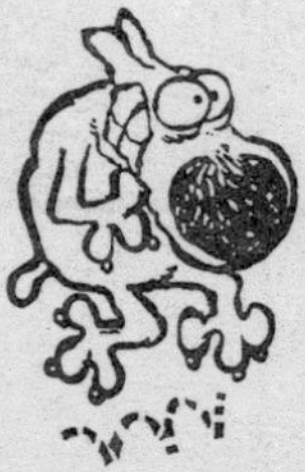

EELS

SNIF
SNIF
SNIF...

PUT A LITTLE HAM, CHEESE, BOLOGNA, LETTUCE 'N' ONIONS BETWEEN SOME BREAD...

10-3

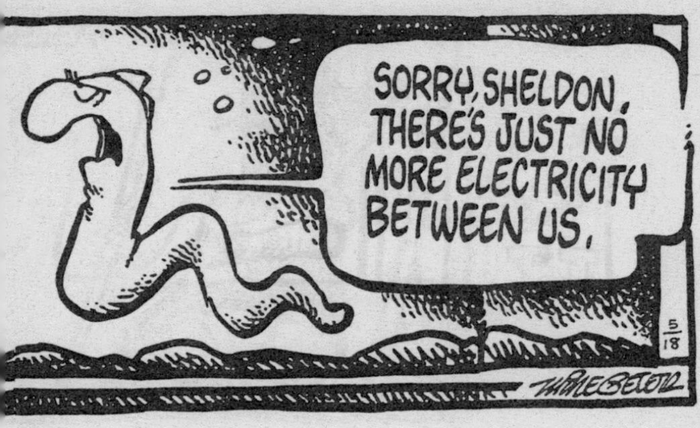
SORRY, SHELDON. THERE'S JUST NO MORE ELECTRICITY BETWEEN US.
5/18

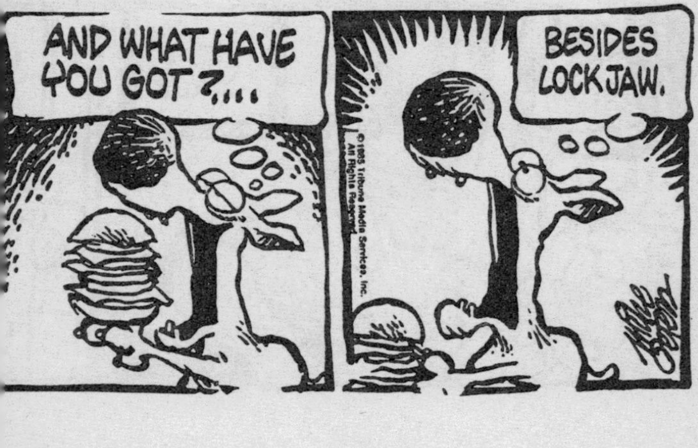
AND WHAT HAVE YOU GOT?...
BESIDES LOCKJAW.
© 1985 Tribune Media Services, Inc.
All Rights Reserved

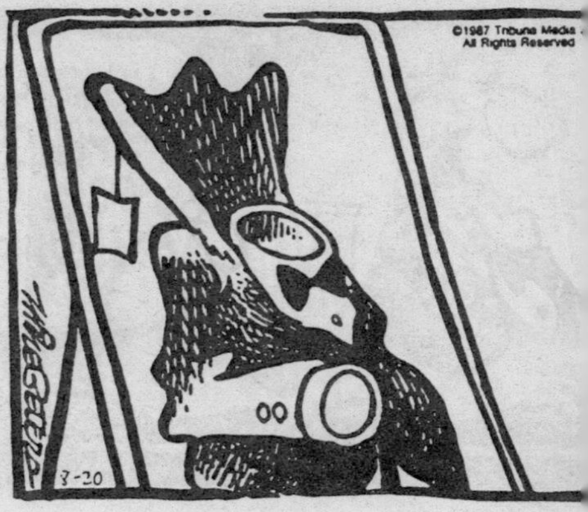
©1987 Tribune Media
All Rights Reserved
8-20

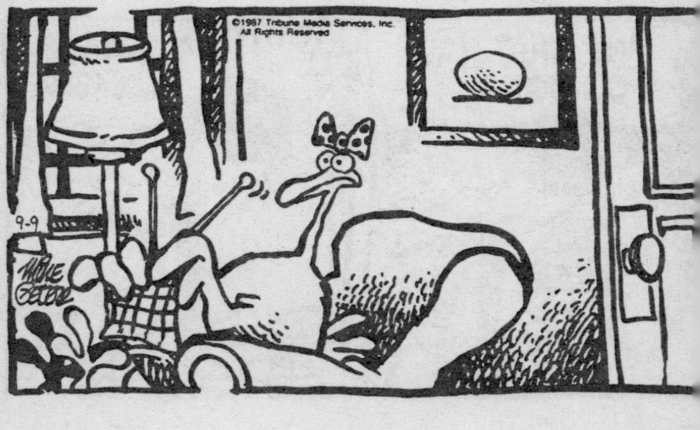
©1987 Tribune Media Services, Inc.
All Rights Reserved
9-9

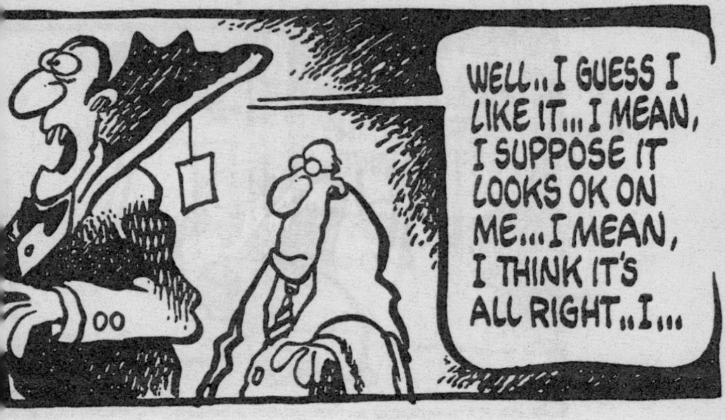
WELL.. I GUESS I LIKE IT... I MEAN, I SUPPOSE IT LOOKS OK ON ME... I MEAN, I THINK IT'S ALL RIGHT.. I...
OO

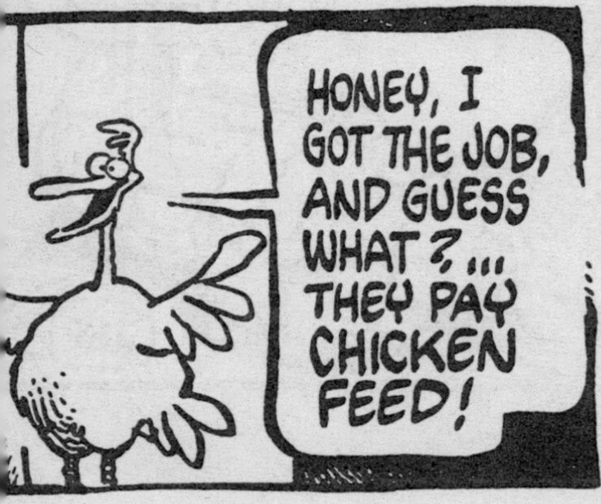
HONEY, I GOT THE JOB, AND GUESS WHAT?... THEY PAY CHICKEN FEED!

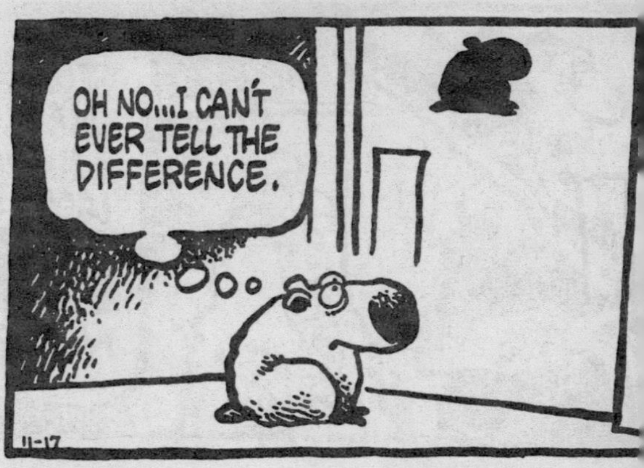
OH NO...I CAN'T EVER TELL THE DIFFERENCE.
11-17

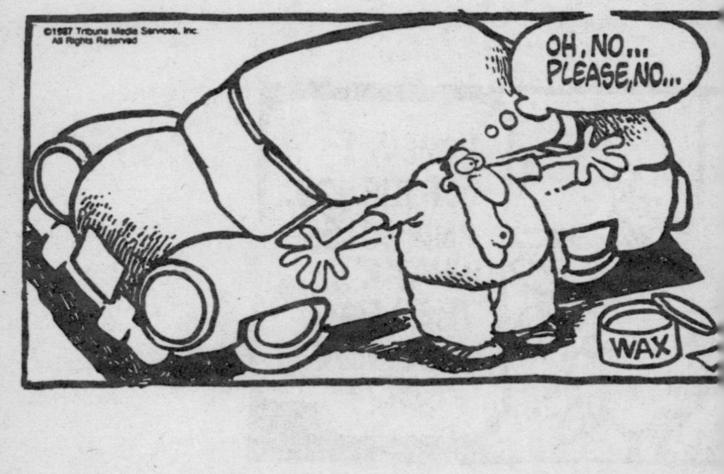
©1987 Tribune Media Services, Inc. All Rights Reserved
OH, NO... PLEASE, NO...
WAX

GERBIL RESTROOMS

8-10

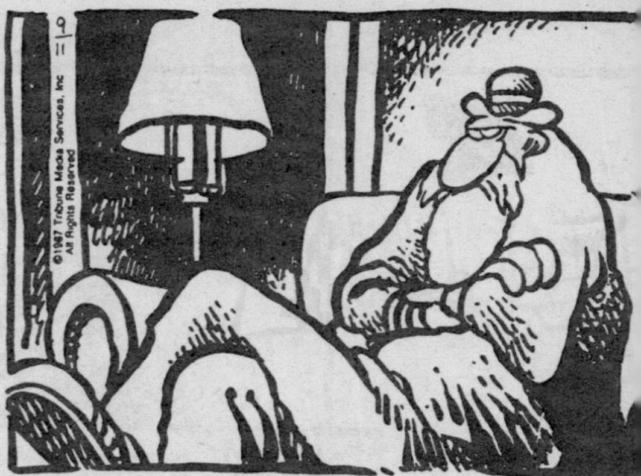
9/11
©1987 Tribune Media Services, Inc
All Rights Reserved

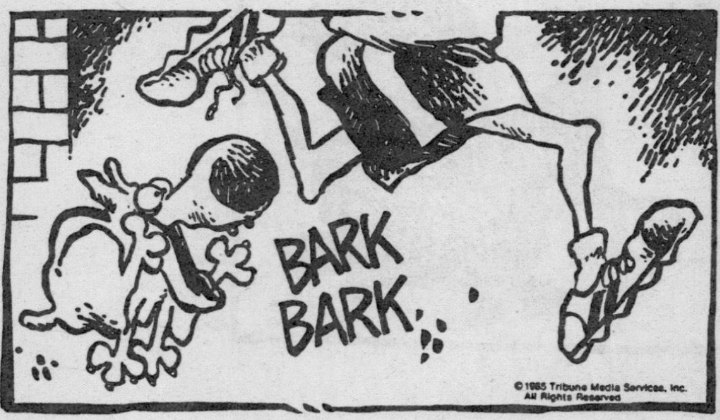
BARK
BARK
©1985 Tribune Media Services, Inc.
All Rights Reserved

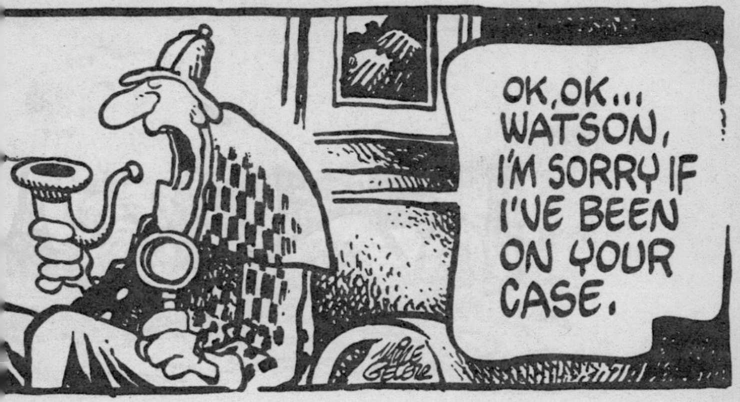
OK,OK... WATSON, I'M SORRY IF I'VE BEEN ON YOUR CASE.
MIKE GEFERE

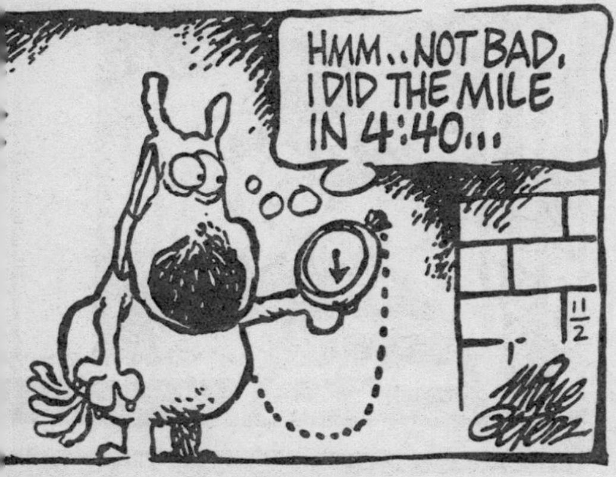
HMM..NOT BAD, I DID THE MILE IN 4:40...
11/2
MIKE GEFERE

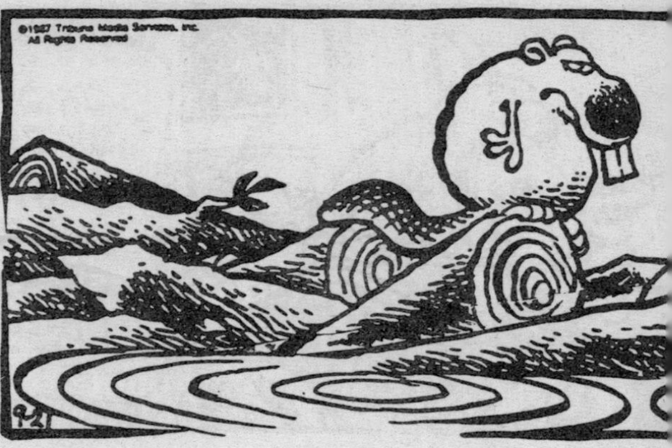
©1987 Tribune Media Services, Inc.
All Rights Reserved
9/21

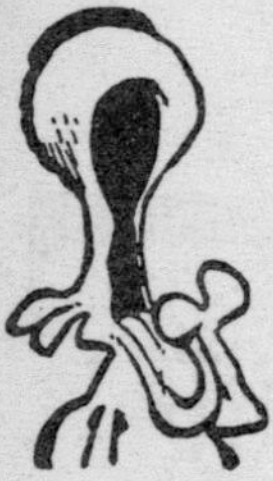

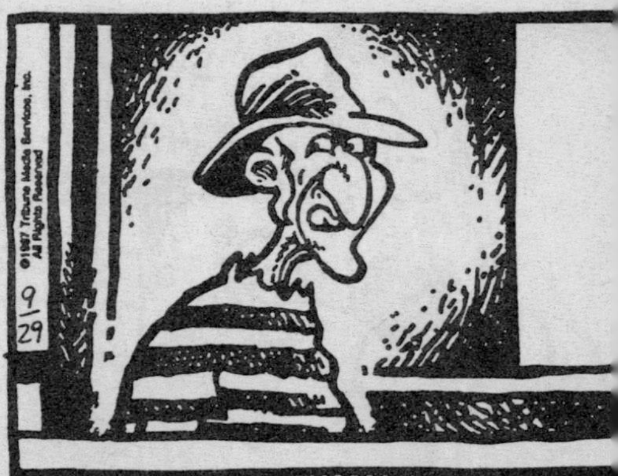
©1987 Tribune Media Services, Inc.
All Rights Reserved
9/29

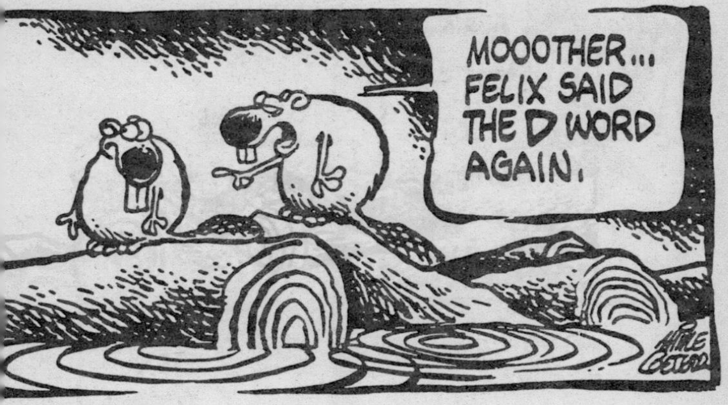
MOOOTHER... FELIX SAID THE D WORD AGAIN.

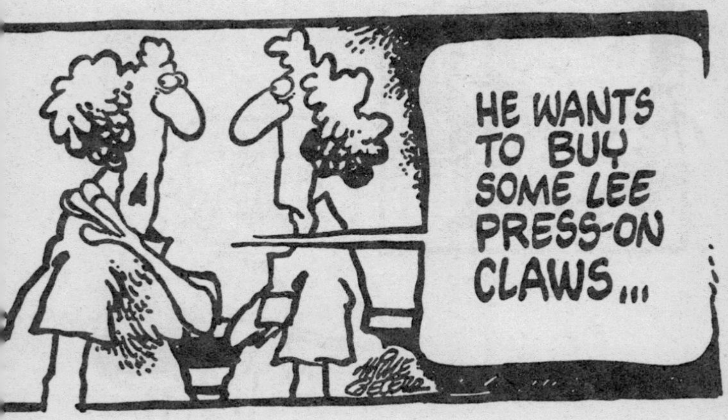
HE WANTS TO BUY SOME LEE PRESS-ON CLAWS...

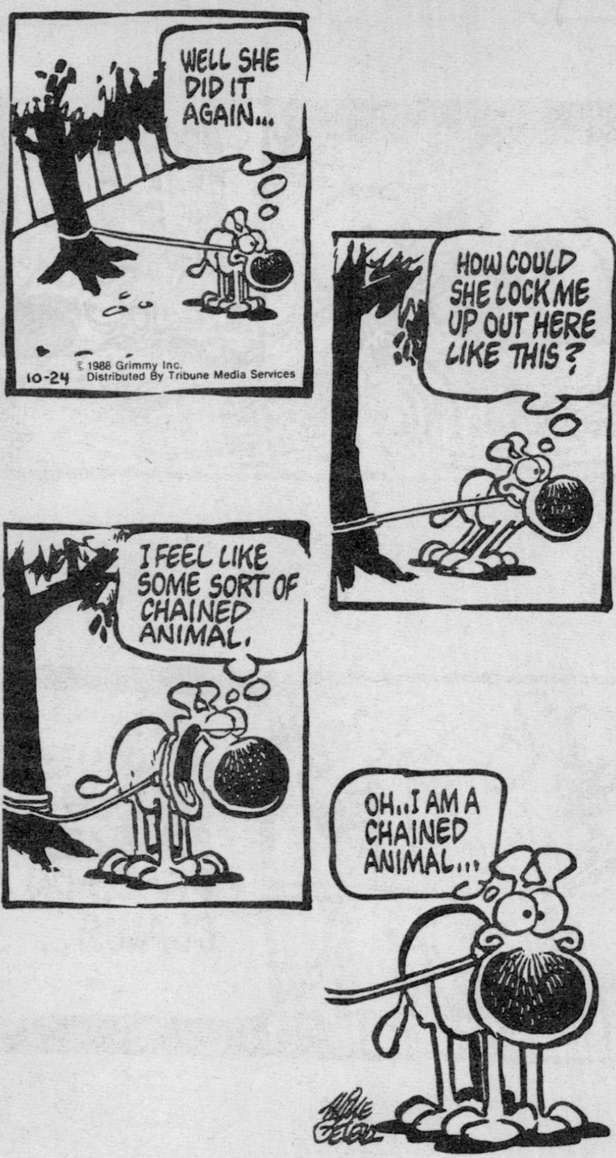
WELL SHE DID IT AGAIN...
10-24
© 1988 Grimmy Inc.
Distributed By Tribune Media Services
HOW COULD SHE LOCK ME UP OUT HERE LIKE THIS?
I FEEL LIKE SOME SORT OF CHAINED ANIMAL.
OH..I AM A CHAINED ANIMAL...

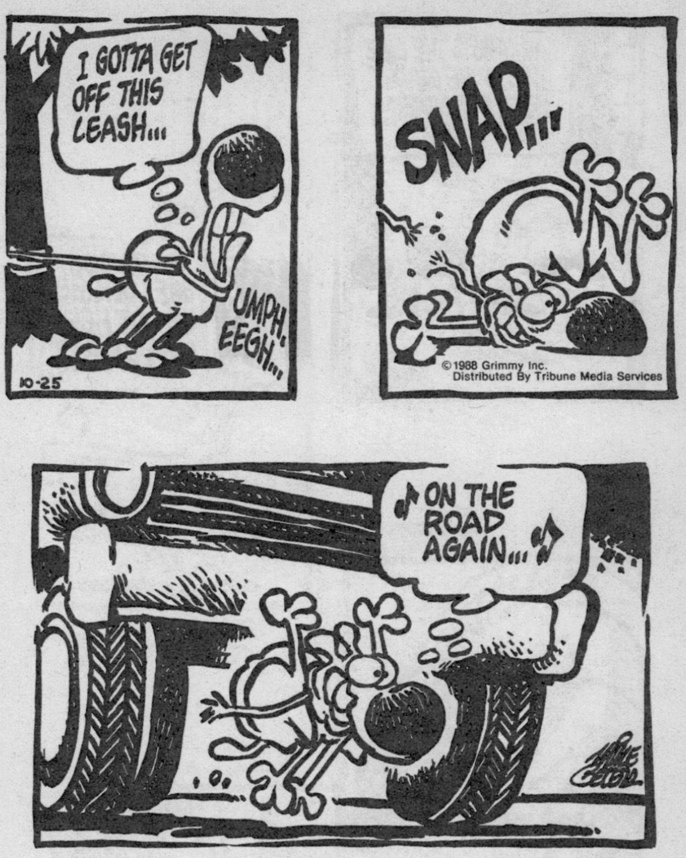
I GOTTA GET OFF THIS LEASH...
UMPH. EEGH...
10-25
SNAP...
© 1988 Grimmy Inc.
Distributed By Tribune Media Services
ON THE ROAD AGAIN...

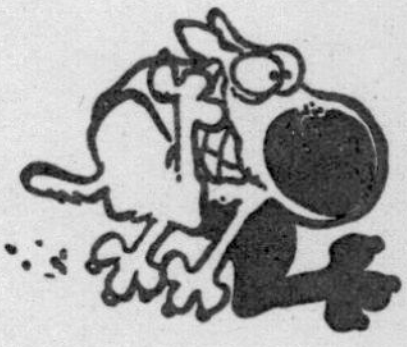

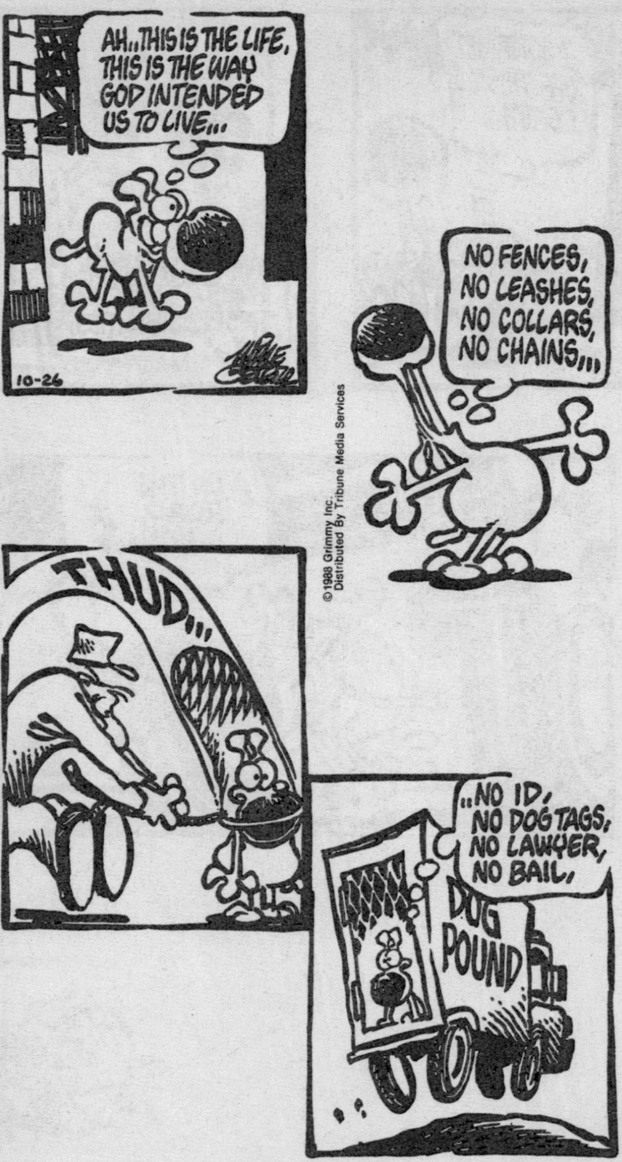
AH..THIS IS THE LIFE, THIS IS THE WAY GOD INTENDED US TO LIVE...
10-26
NO FENCES, NO LEASHES, NO COLLARS, NO CHAINS,...
THUD,,,
..NO ID, NO DOG TAGS, NO LAWYER, NO BAIL,
DOG POUND

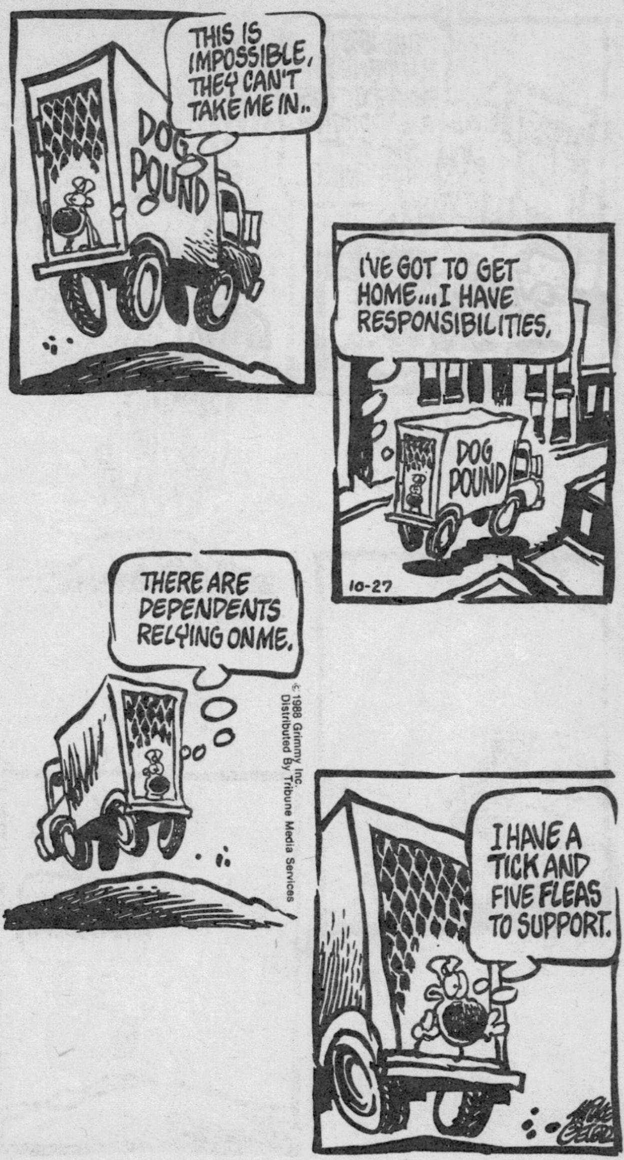
THIS IS IMPOSSIBLE, THEY CAN'T TAKE ME IN..
DOG POUND
I'VE GOT TO GET HOME...I HAVE RESPONSIBILITIES.
DOG POUND
10-27
THERE ARE DEPENDENTS RELYING ON ME.
I HAVE A TICK AND FIVE FLEAS TO SUPPORT.
MIKE PETERS

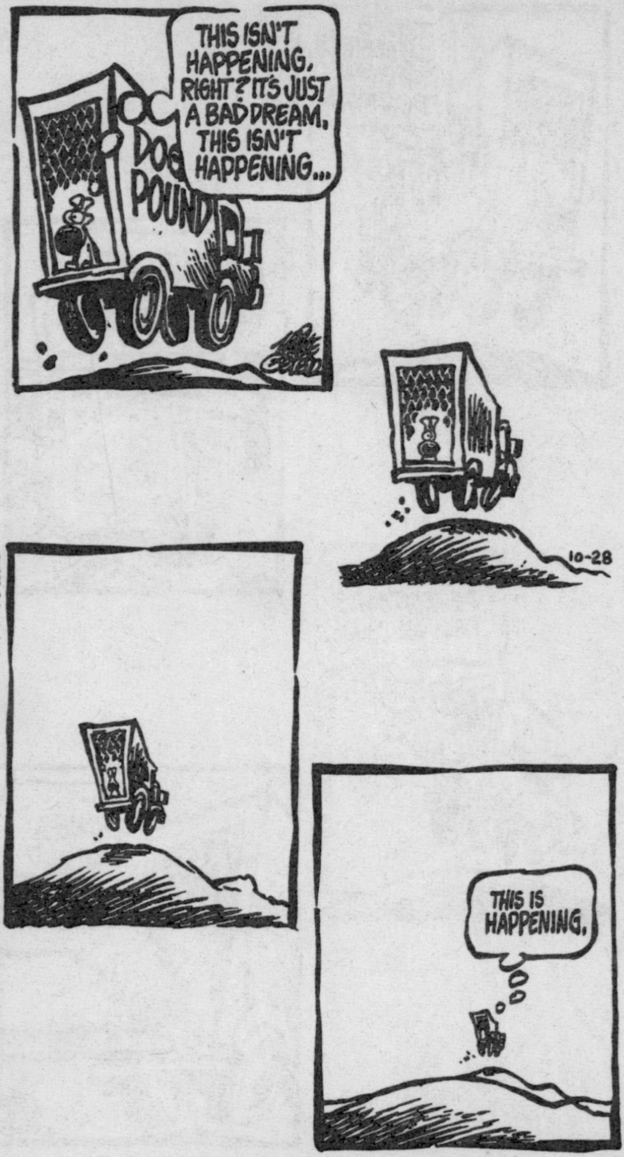
THIS ISN'T HAPPENING, RIGHT? IT'S JUST A BAD DREAM, THIS ISN'T HAPPENING...
DOG POUND
10-28
THIS IS HAPPENING.

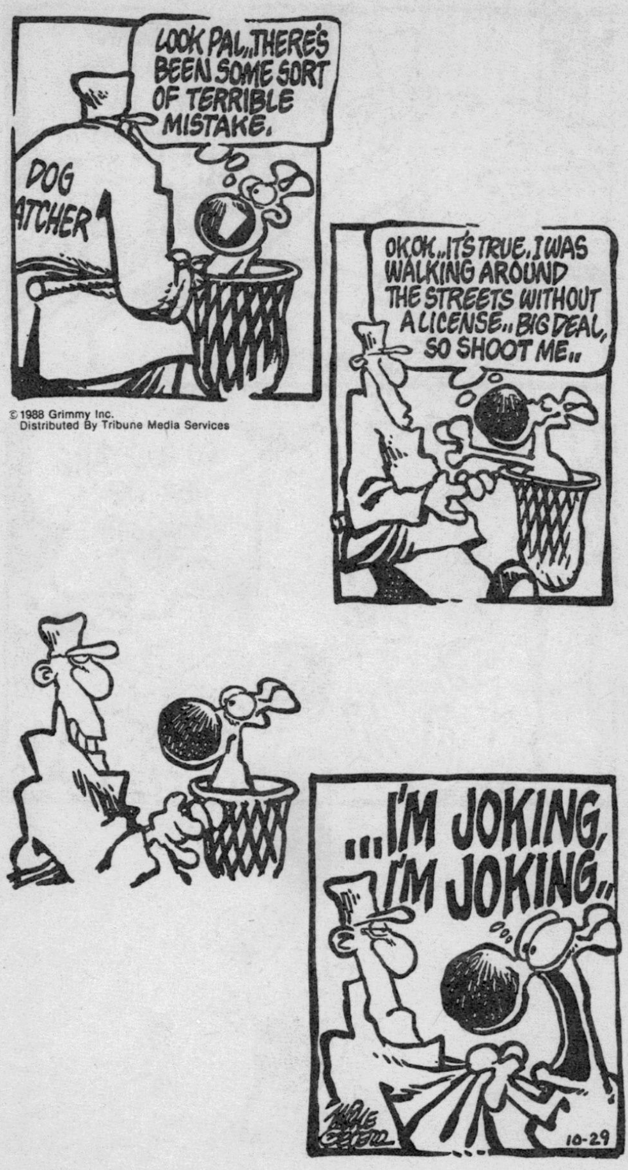
LOOK PAL..THERE'S BEEN SOME SORT OF TERRIBLE MISTAKE.
DOG ATCHER
OK,OK..IT'S TRUE, I WAS WALKING AROUND THE STREETS WITHOUT A LICENSE.. BIG DEAL, SO SHOOT ME..
...I'M JOKING, I'M JOKING..
10-29

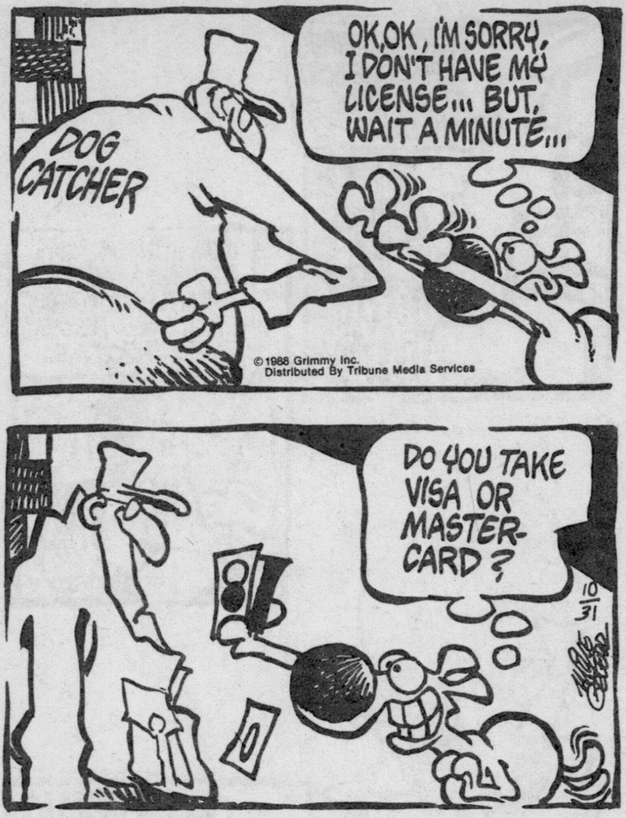
OK,OK, I'M SORRY, I DON'T HAVE MY LICENSE... BUT, WAIT A MINUTE...
DOG CATCHER
© 1988 Grimmy Inc.
Distributed By Tribune Media Services
DO YOU TAKE VISA OR MASTER-CARD?
10/31

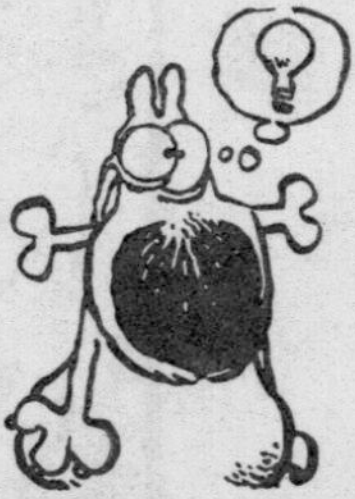

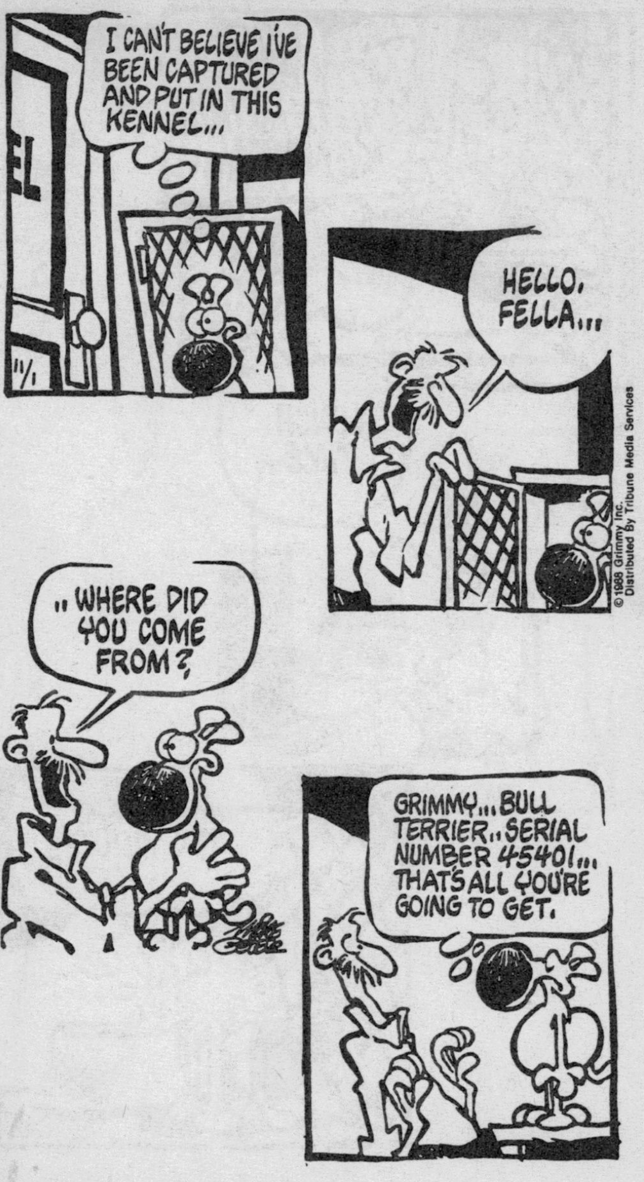
I CAN'T BELIEVE I'VE BEEN CAPTURED AND PUT IN THIS KENNEL...
11/1
HELLO, FELLA...
© 1988 Grimmy Inc. Distributed By Tribune Media Services
.. WHERE DID YOU COME FROM?
GRIMMY... BULL TERRIER.. SERIAL NUMBER 45401... THAT'S ALL YOU'RE GOING TO GET.

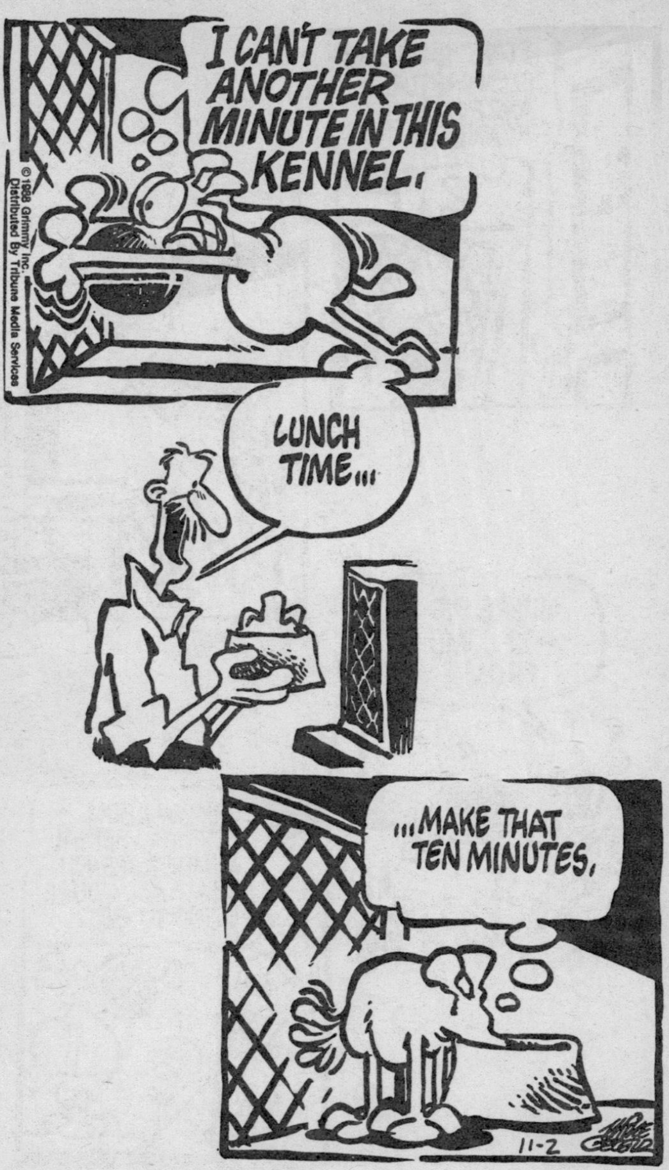
I CAN'T TAKE ANOTHER MINUTE IN THIS KENNEL.
© 1988 Grimmy Inc. Distributed By Tribune Media Services
LUNCH TIME...
...MAKE THAT TEN MINUTES.
11-2

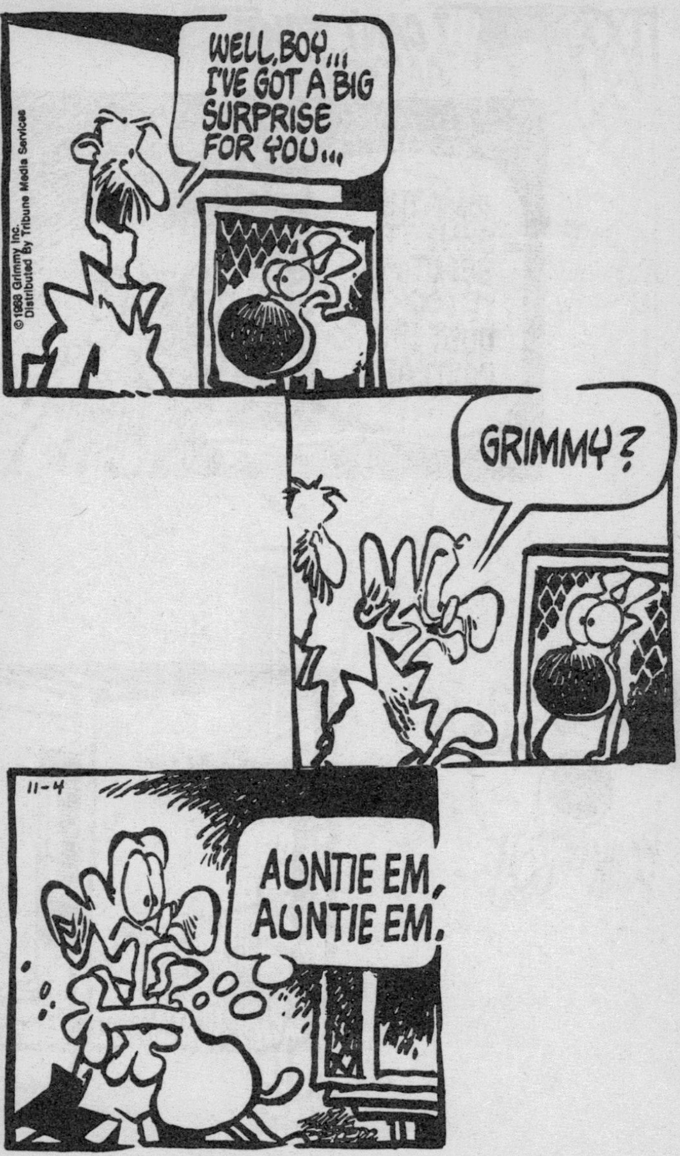
WELL, BOY... I'VE GOT A BIG SURPRISE FOR YOU...
© 1988 Grimmy Inc. Distributed By Tribune Media Services
GRIMMY?
11-4
AUNTIE EM, AUNTIE EM.

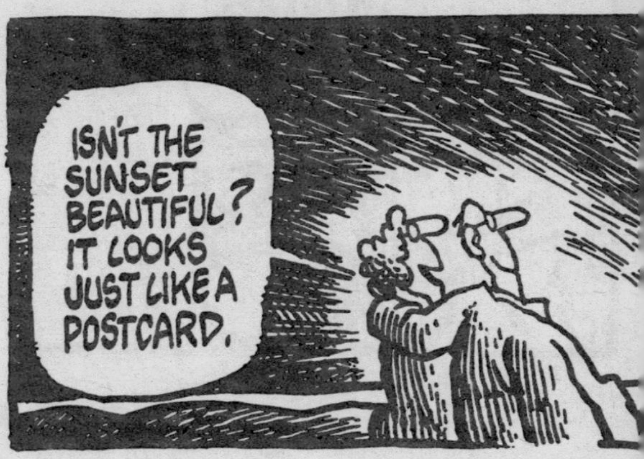
ISN'T THE SUNSET BEAUTIFUL? IT LOOKS JUST LIKE A POSTCARD.

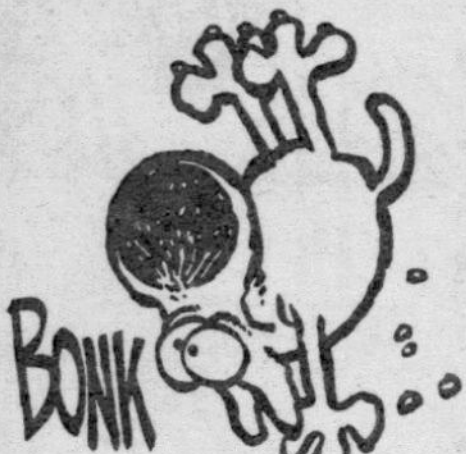
BONK

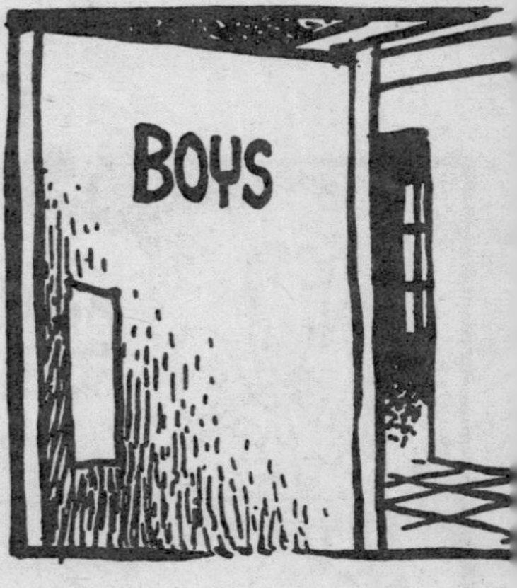
BOYS

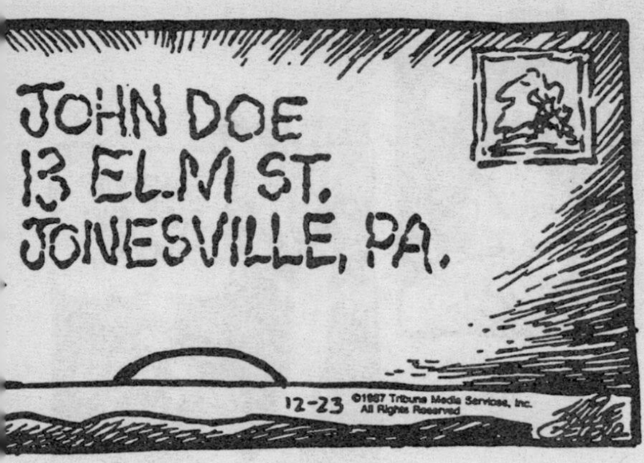
JOHN DOE
13 ELM ST.
JONESVILLE, PA.
12-23
©1987 Tribune Media Services, Inc.
All Rights Reserved

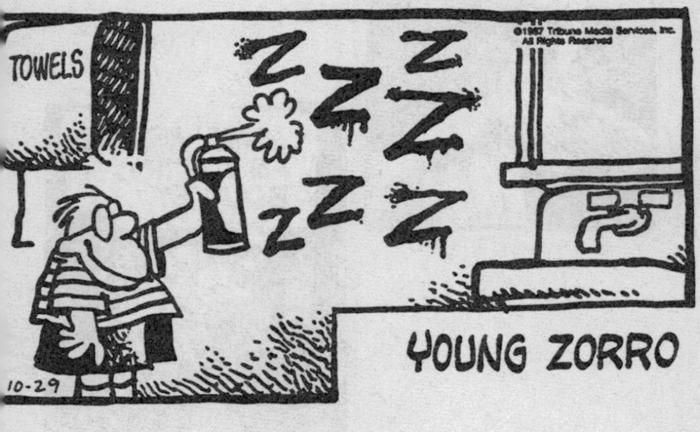
TOWELS
ZZZ
ZZ
ZZZ
©1987 Tribune Media Services, Inc.
All Rights Reserved
10-29

YOUNG ZORRO

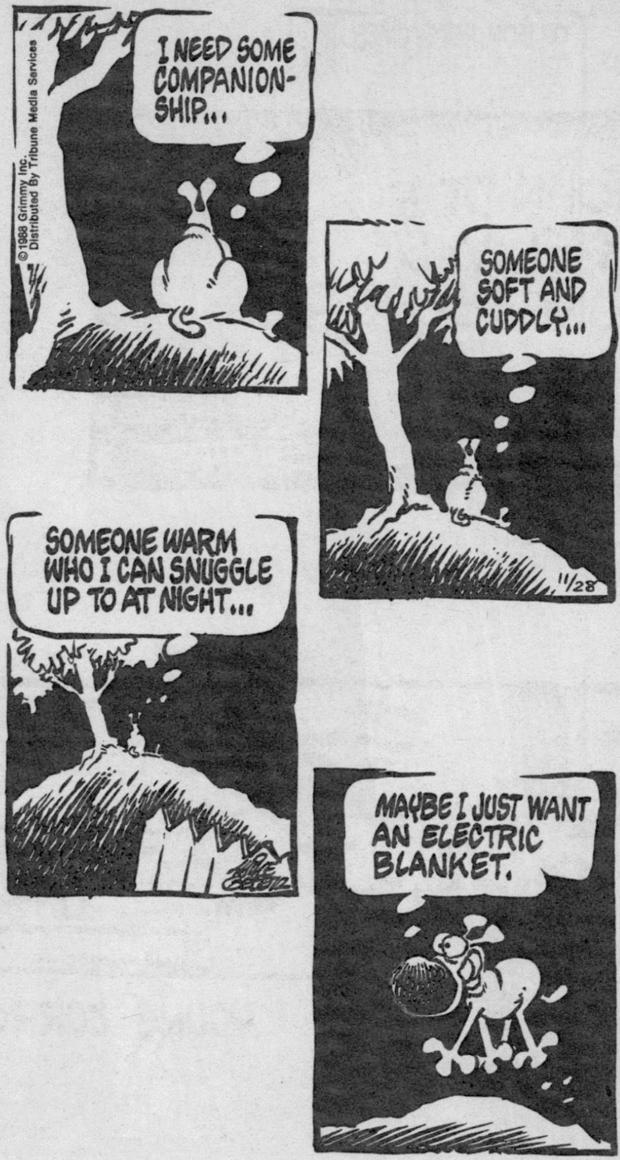
© 1988 Grimmy Inc.
Distributed By Tribune Media Services
I NEED SOME COMPANIONSHIP...
SOMEONE SOFT AND CUDDLY...
11/28
SOMEONE WARM WHO I CAN SNUGGLE UP TO AT NIGHT...
MAYBE I JUST WANT AN ELECTRIC BLANKET.

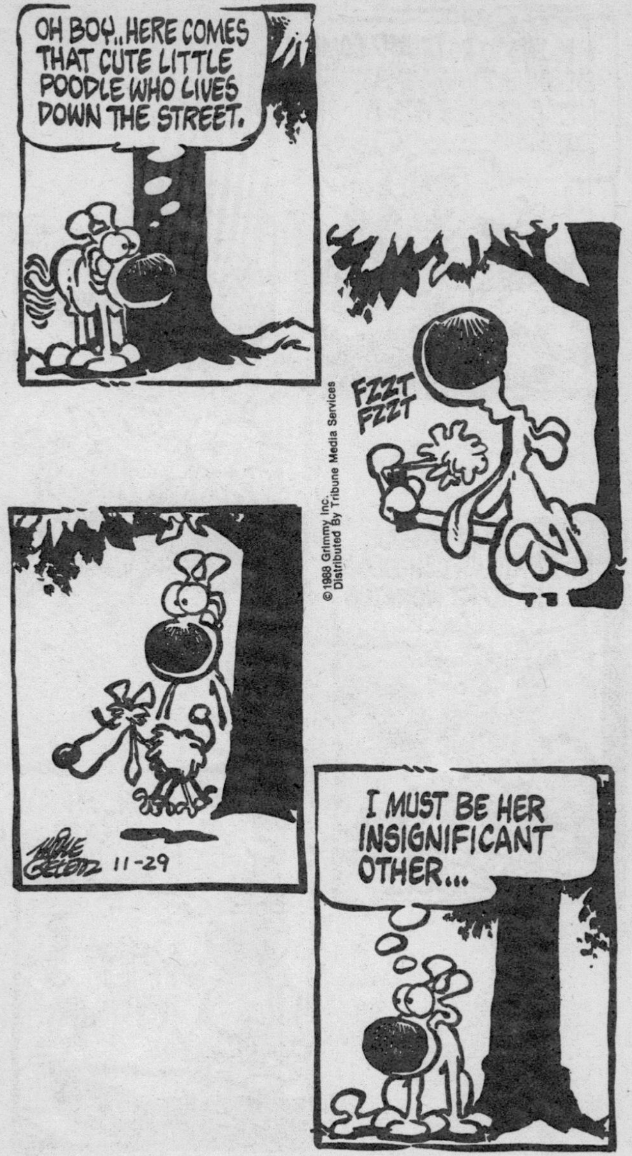

OH BOY.. HERE COMES THAT CUTE LITTLE POODLE WHO LIVES DOWN THE STREET.
FZZT FZZT
11-29
I MUST BE HER INSIGNIFICANT OTHER...

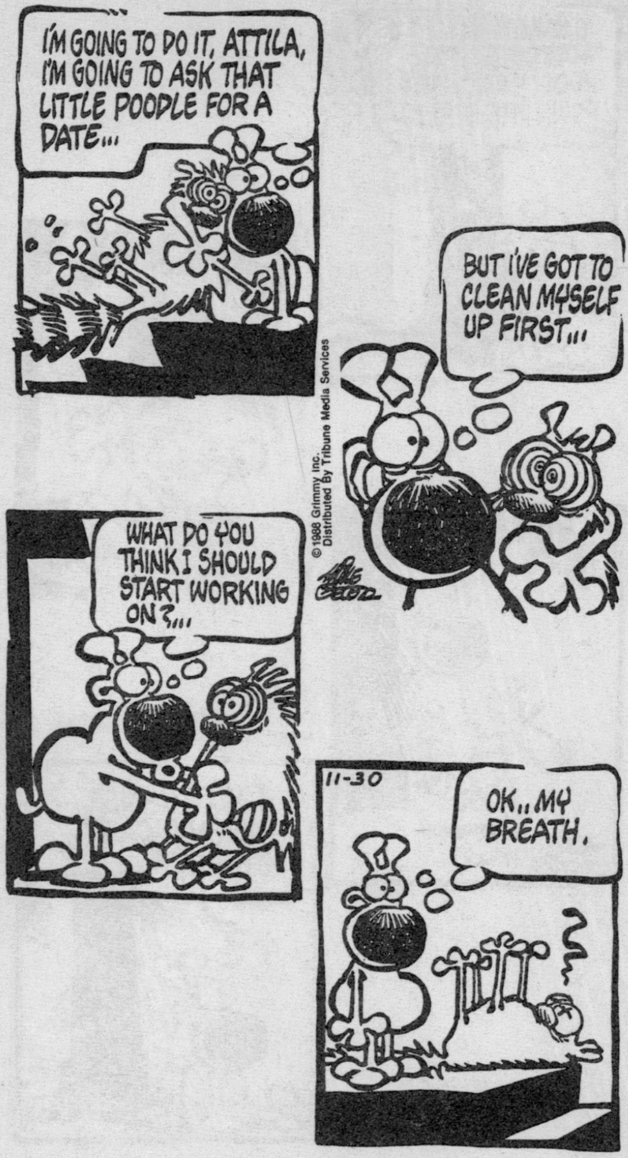

I'M GOING TO DO IT, ATTILA, I'M GOING TO ASK THAT LITTLE POODLE FOR A DATE...
BUT I'VE GOT TO CLEAN MYSELF UP FIRST...
© 1988 Grimmy Inc.
Distributed By Tribune Media Services
WHAT DO YOU THINK I SHOULD START WORKING ON?...
11-30
OK.. MY BREATH.

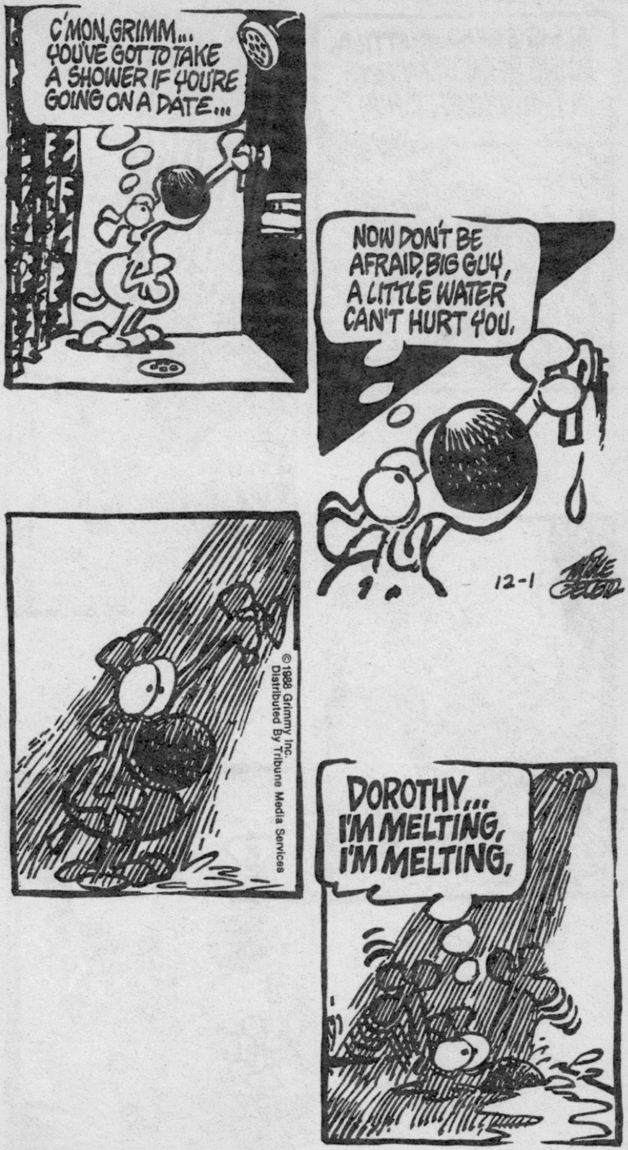
C'MON, GRIMM... YOU'VE GOT TO TAKE A SHOWER IF YOU'RE GOING ON A DATE...
NOW DON'T BE AFRAID, BIG GUY, A LITTLE WATER CAN'T HURT YOU.
12-1
© 1988 Grimmy Inc. Distributed By Tribune Media Services
DOROTHY... I'M MELTING, I'M MELTING,

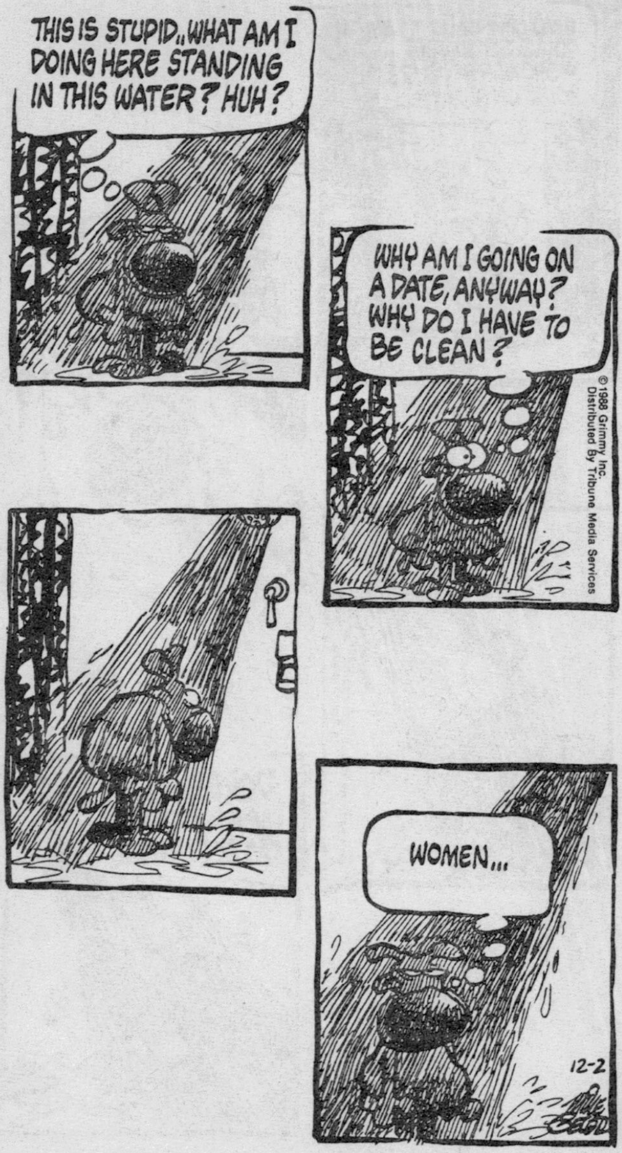
THIS IS STUPID.. WHAT AM I DOING HERE STANDING IN THIS WATER? HUH?
WHY AM I GOING ON A DATE, ANYWAY? WHY DO I HAVE TO BE CLEAN?
© 1988 Grimmy Inc.
Distributed By Tribune Media Services
WOMEN...
12-2
MIKE PETERS

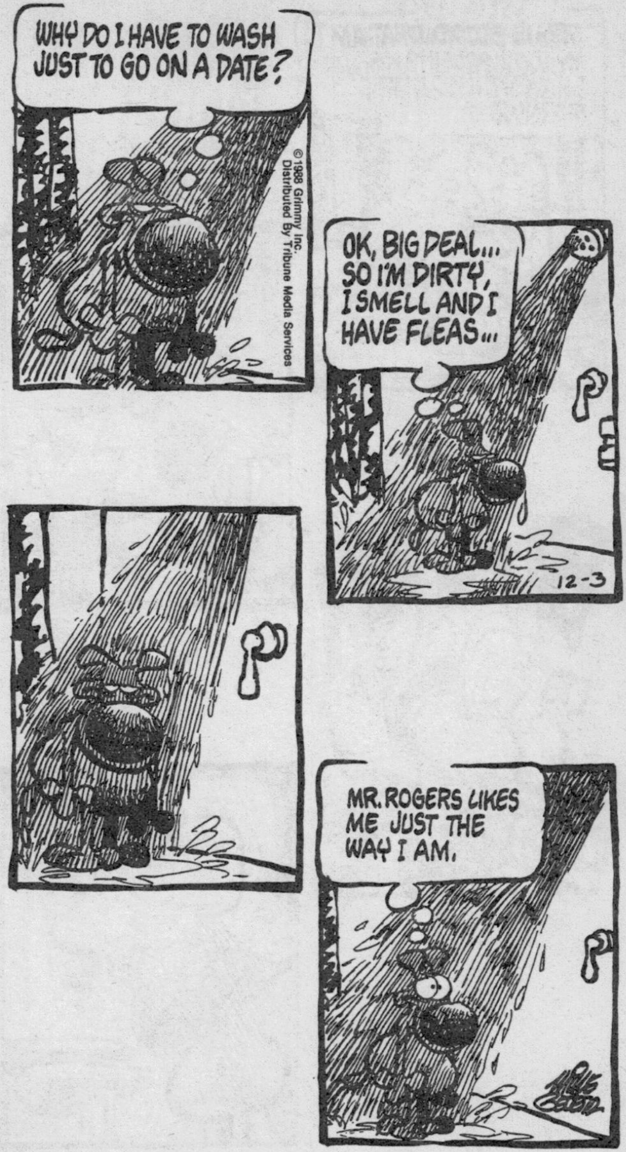
WHY DO I HAVE TO WASH JUST TO GO ON A DATE?
© 1988 Grimmy Inc. Distributed By Tribune Media Services
OK, BIG DEAL... SO I'M DIRTY, I SMELL AND I HAVE FLEAS...
12-3
MR. ROGERS LIKES ME JUST THE WAY I AM.

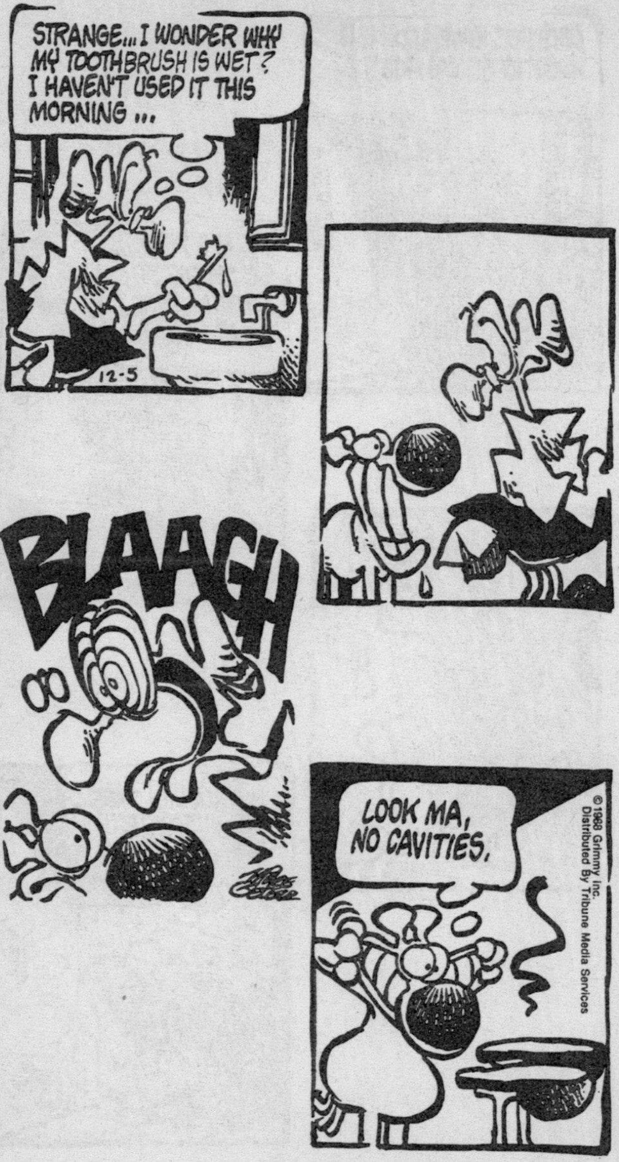
STRANGE... I WONDER WHY MY TOOTHBRUSH IS WET? I HAVEN'T USED IT THIS MORNING ...
12-5
BLAAGH
LOOK MA, NO CAVITIES.
© 1988 Grimmy Inc. Distributed By Tribune Media Services

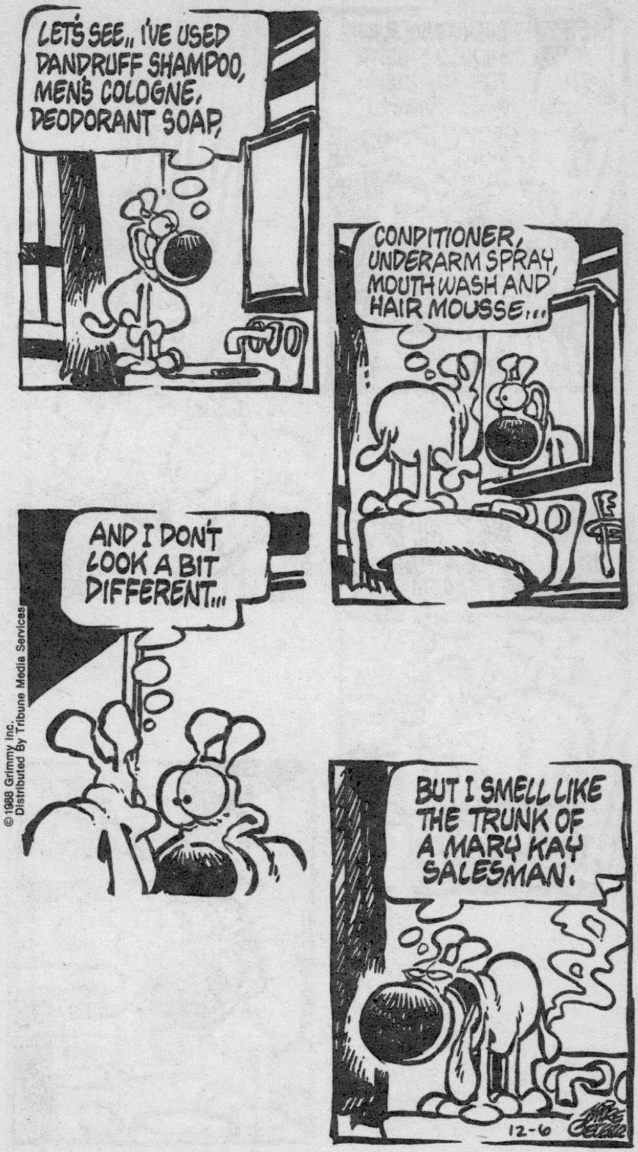
LET'S SEE.. I'VE USED DANDRUFF SHAMPOO, MEN'S COLOGNE, DEODORANT SOAP,
CONDITIONER, UNDERARM SPRAY, MOUTHWASH AND HAIR MOUSSE...
AND I DON'T LOOK A BIT DIFFERENT...
BUT I SMELL LIKE THE TRUNK OF A MARY KAY SALESMAN.
12-6
© 1988 Grimmy Inc.
Distributed By Tribune Media Services

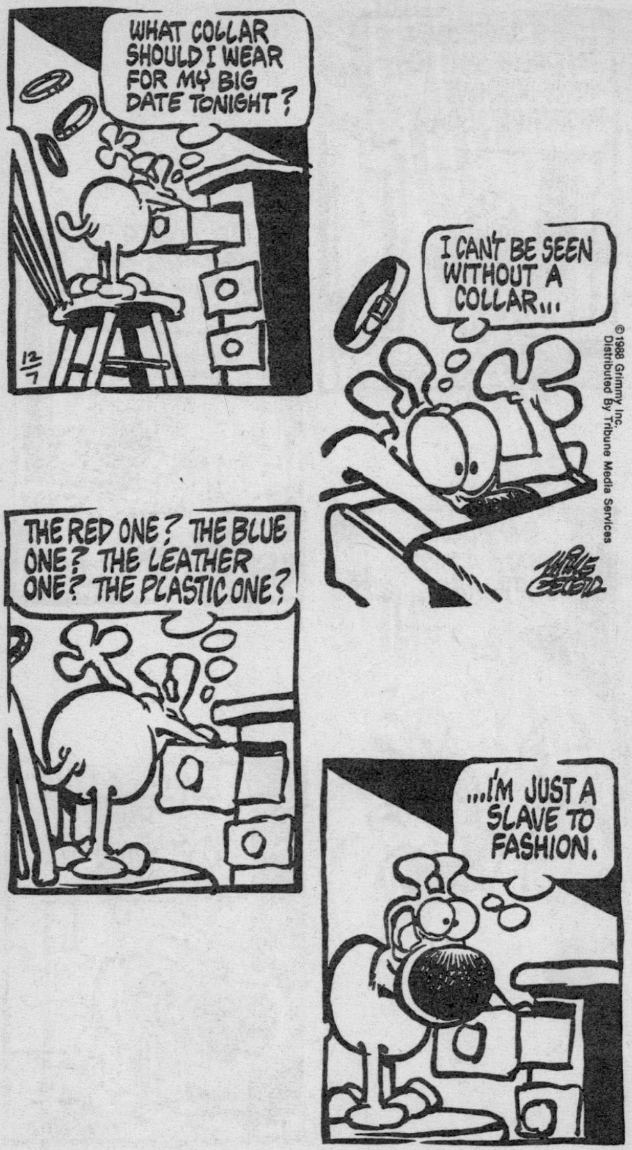
WHAT COLLAR SHOULD I WEAR FOR MY BIG DATE TONIGHT?
12/7
THE RED ONE? THE BLUE ONE? THE LEATHER ONE? THE PLASTIC ONE?
I CAN'T BE SEEN WITHOUT A COLLAR...
...I'M JUST A SLAVE TO FASHION.
© 1988 Grimmy Inc. Distributed By Tribune Media Services

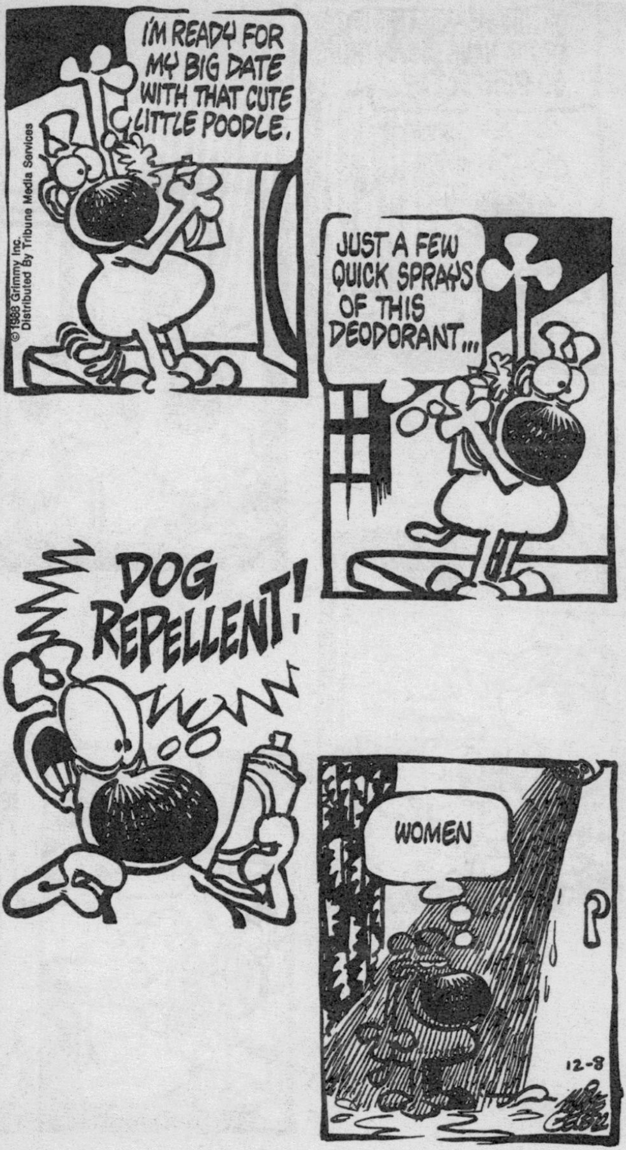
I'M READY FOR MY BIG DATE WITH THAT CUTE LITTLE POODLE.
©1988 Grimmy Inc.
Distributed By Tribune Media Services
JUST A FEW QUICK SPRAYS OF THIS DEODORANT...
DOG REPELLENT!
WOMEN
12-8

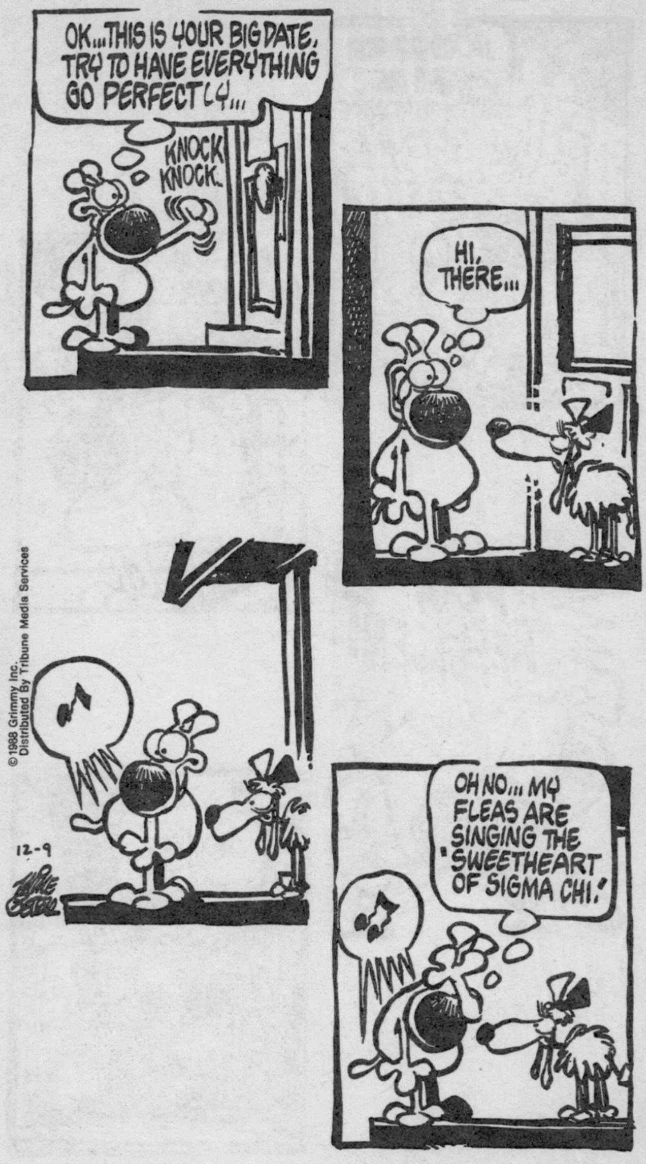
OK...THIS IS YOUR BIG DATE. TRY TO HAVE EVERYTHING GO PERFECTLY...
KNOCK KNOCK...
HI, THERE...
OH NO... MY FLEAS ARE SINGING THE "SWEETHEART OF SIGMA CHI."
12-9

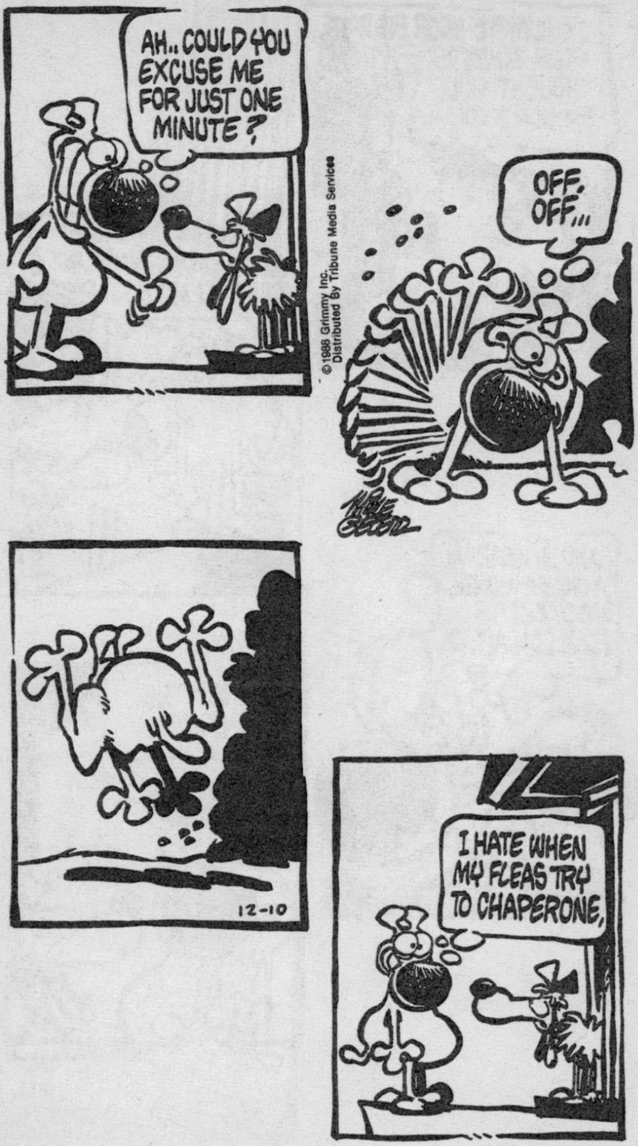
AH.. COULD YOU EXCUSE ME FOR JUST ONE MINUTE?
OFF. OFF...
I HATE WHEN MY FLEAS TRY TO CHAPERONE.
12-10
© 1988 Grimmy Inc.
Distributed By Tribune Media Services

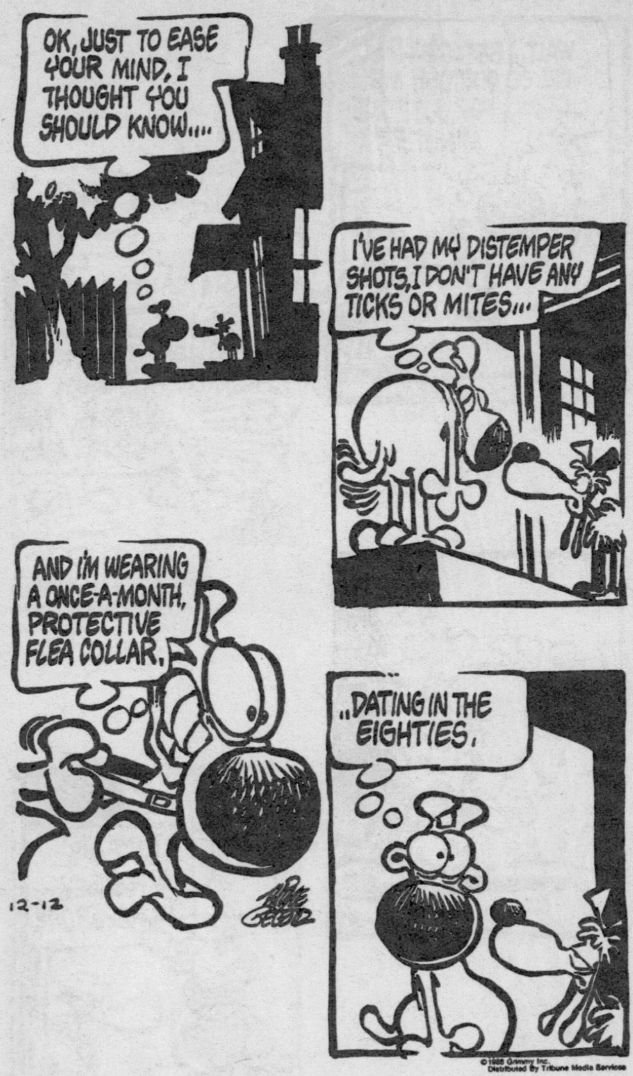
OK, JUST TO EASE YOUR MIND, I THOUGHT YOU SHOULD KNOW....
I'VE HAD MY DISTEMPER SHOTS, I DON'T HAVE ANY TICKS OR MITES...
AND I'M WEARING A ONCE-A-MONTH, PROTECTIVE FLEA COLLAR.
..DATING IN THE EIGHTIES.
12-12

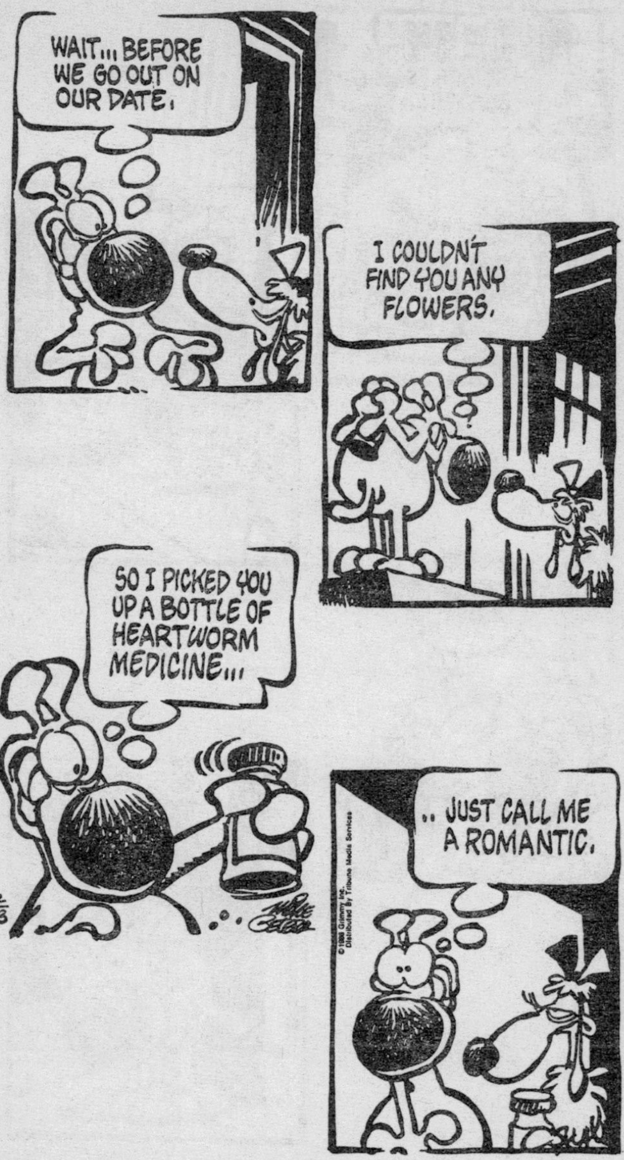
WAIT... BEFORE WE GO OUT ON OUR DATE.
I COULDN'T FIND YOU ANY FLOWERS.
SO I PICKED YOU UP A BOTTLE OF HEARTWORM MEDICINE...
.. JUST CALL ME A ROMANTIC.
12/13
© 1988 Grimmy Inc.
Distributed By Tribune Media Services

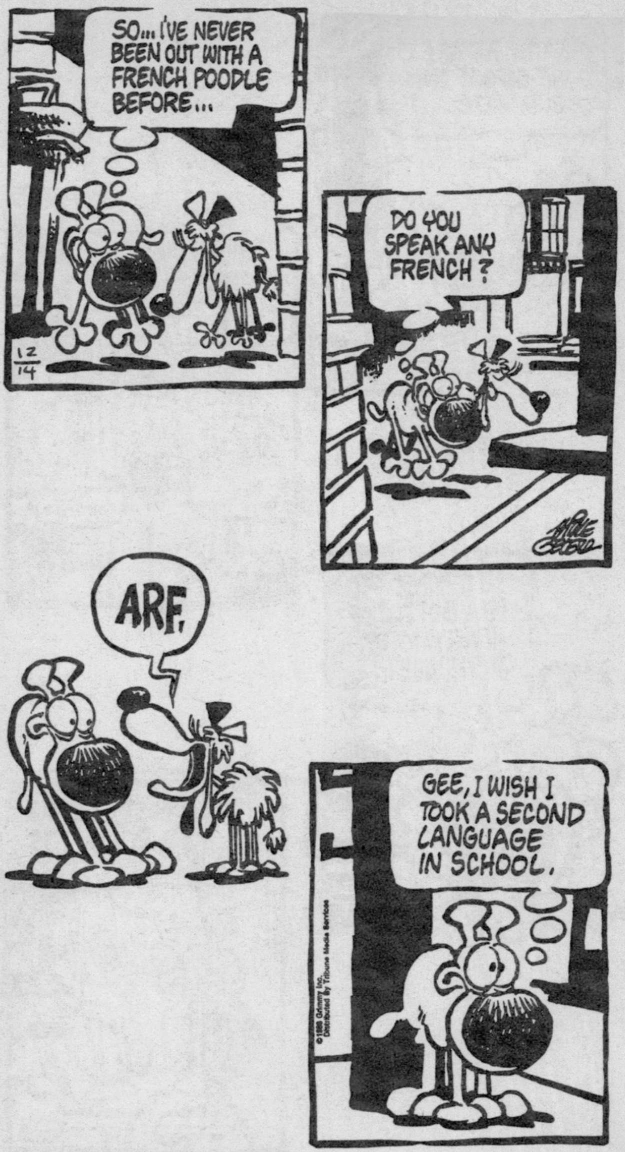
12/14
SO... I'VE NEVER BEEN OUT WITH A FRENCH POODLE BEFORE...
DO YOU SPEAK ANY FRENCH?
ARF.
GEE, I WISH I TOOK A SECOND LANGUAGE IN SCHOOL.
©1988 Grimmy Inc. Distributed by Tribune Media Services

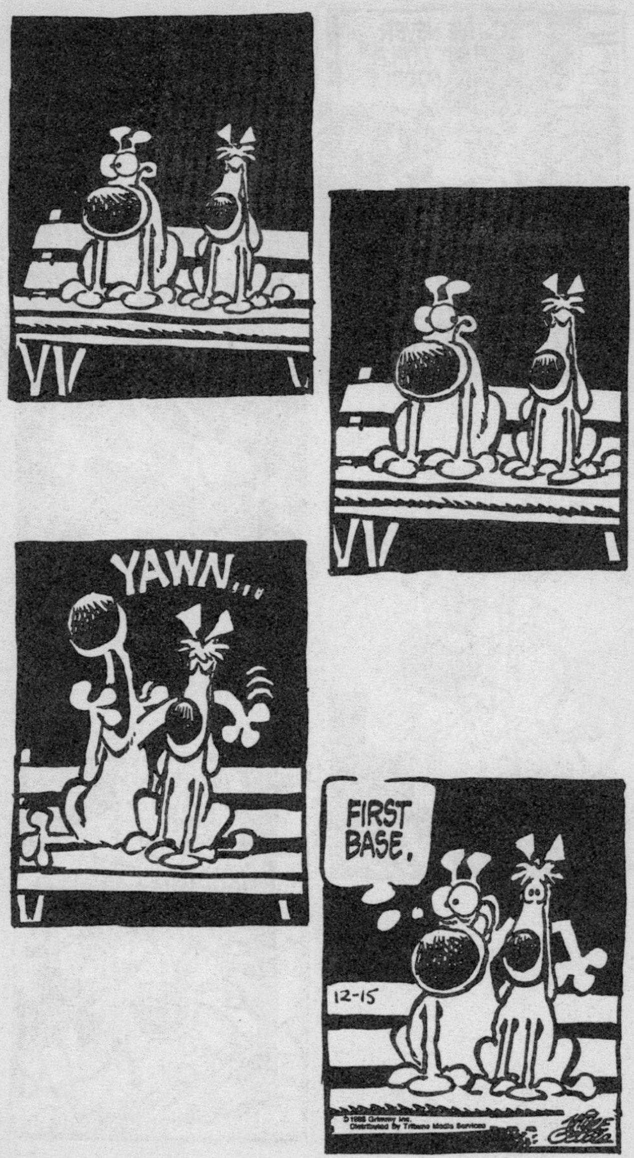
YAWN...
FIRST BASE.
12-15

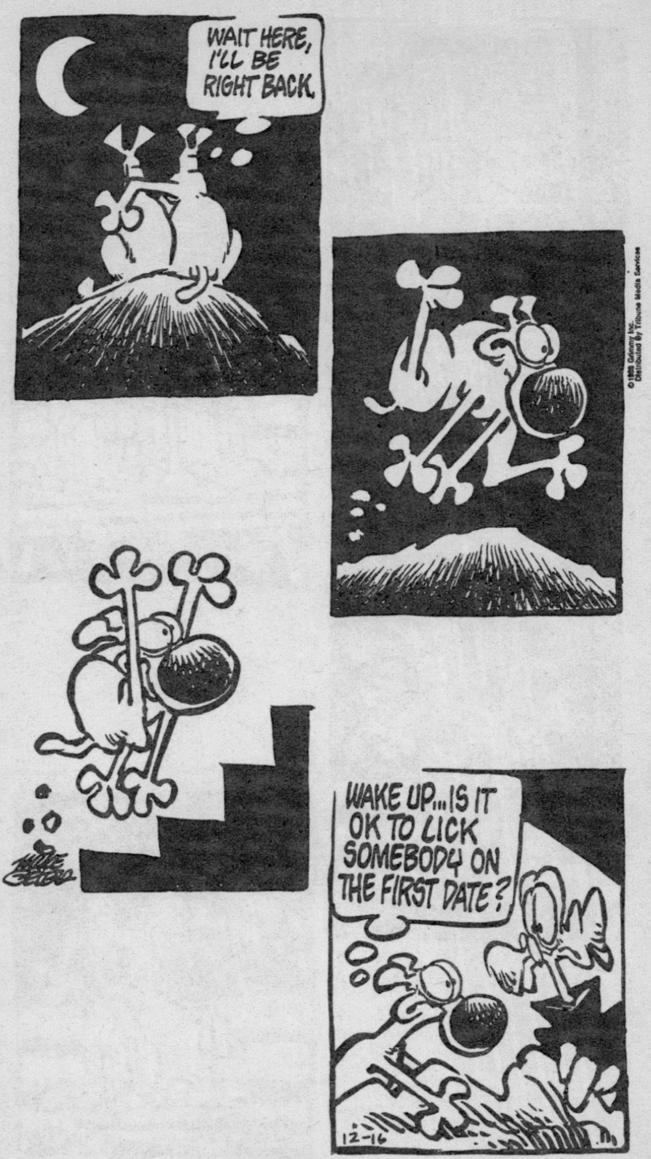
WAIT HERE, I'LL BE RIGHT BACK.
Grimmy Inc.
Distributed By Tribune Media Services
WAKE UP...IS IT OK TO LICK SOMEBODY ON THE FIRST DATE?
12-16

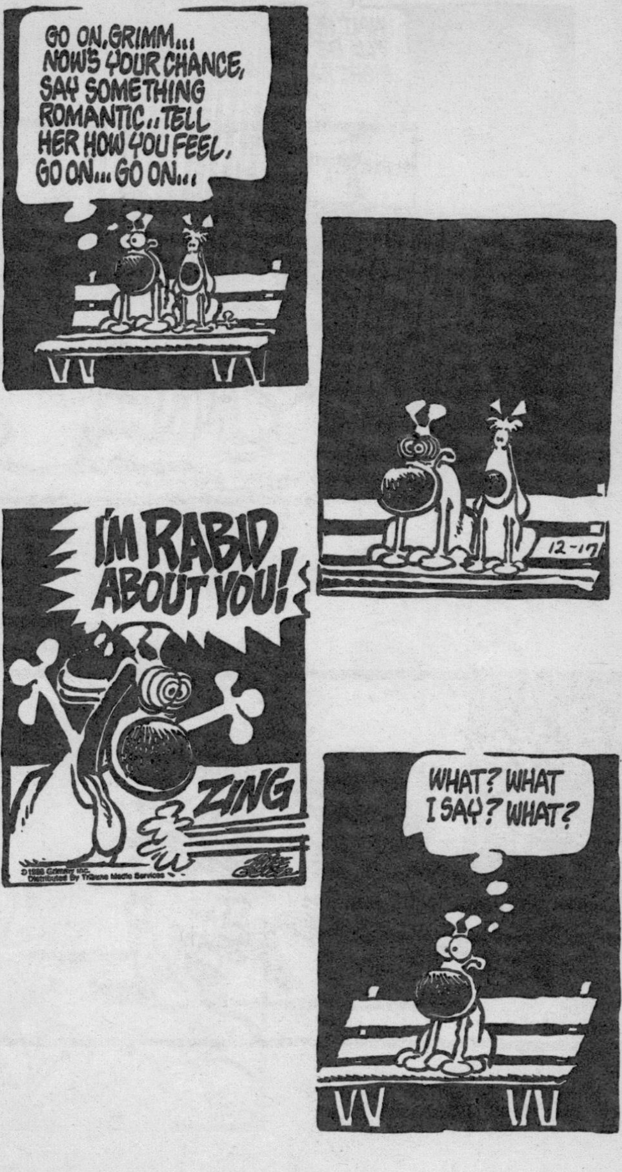
GO ON, GRIMM... NOW'S YOUR CHANCE, SAY SOMETHING ROMANTIC.. TELL HER HOW YOU FEEL. GO ON... GO ON...
12-17
I'M RABID ABOUT YOU!
ZING
Grimmy Inc.
Distributed By Tribune Media Services
WHAT? WHAT I SAY? WHAT?

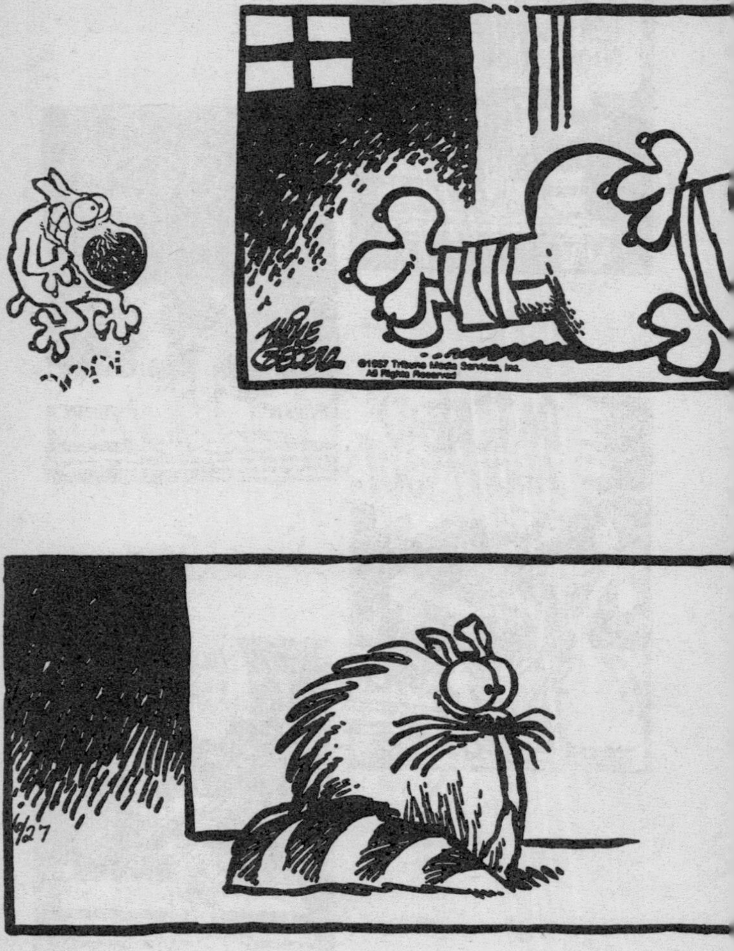
©1987 Tribune Media Services, Inc.
All Rights Reserved

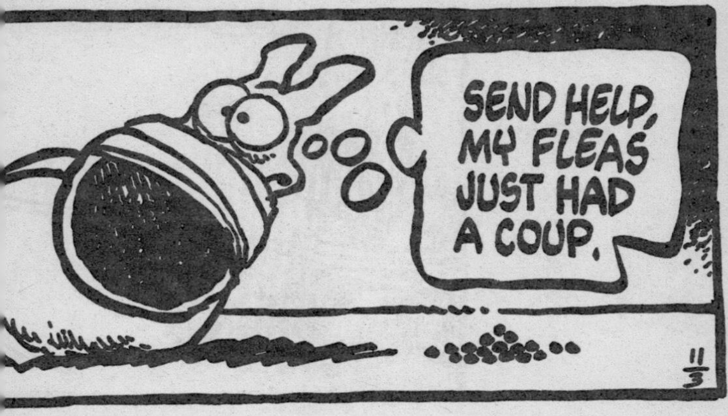
SEND HELP, MY FLEAS JUST HAD A COUP.
11/3

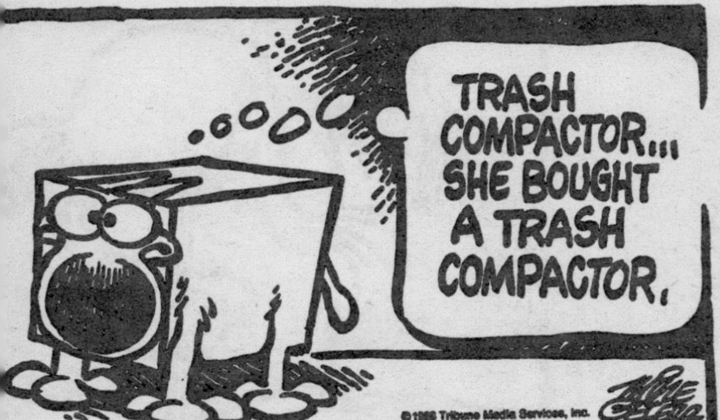
TRASH COMPACTOR... SHE BOUGHT A TRASH COMPACTOR.

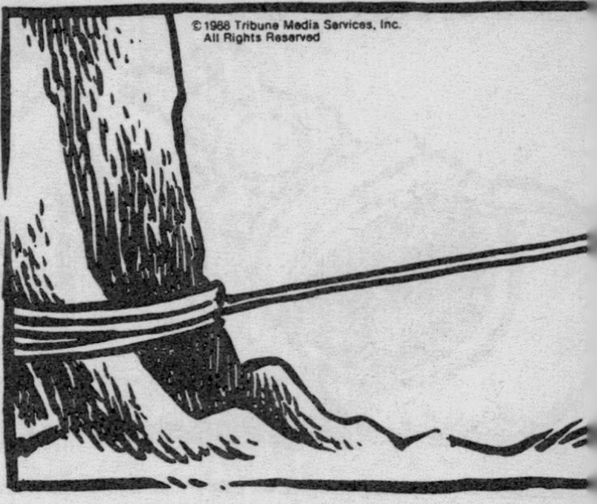
©1988 Tribune Media Services, Inc.
All Rights Reserved

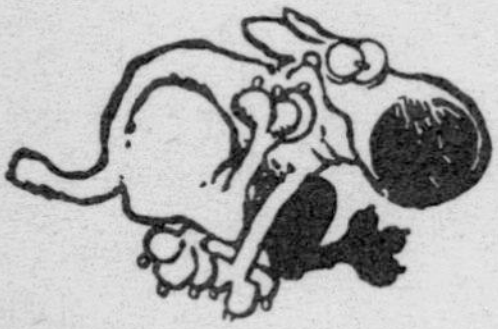

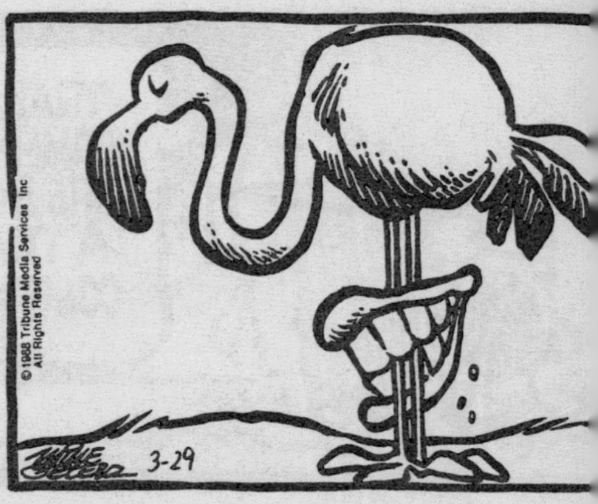
©1988 Tribune Media Services Inc
All Rights Reserved
3-29

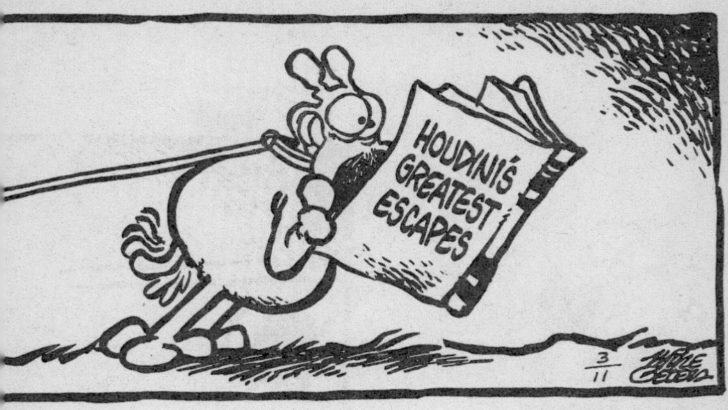
HOUDINI'S GREATEST ESCAPES

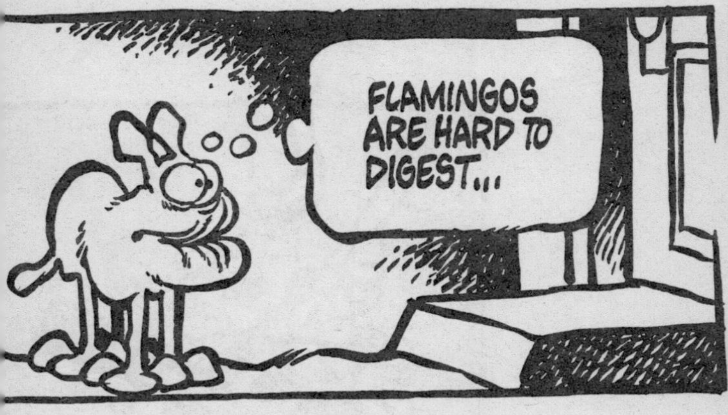
FLAMINGOS ARE HARD TO DIGEST...

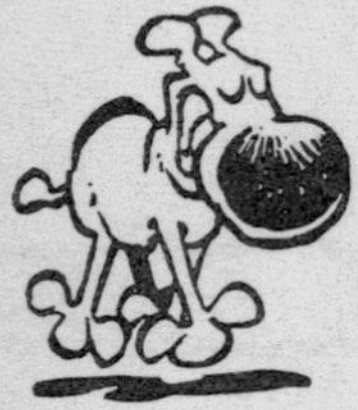

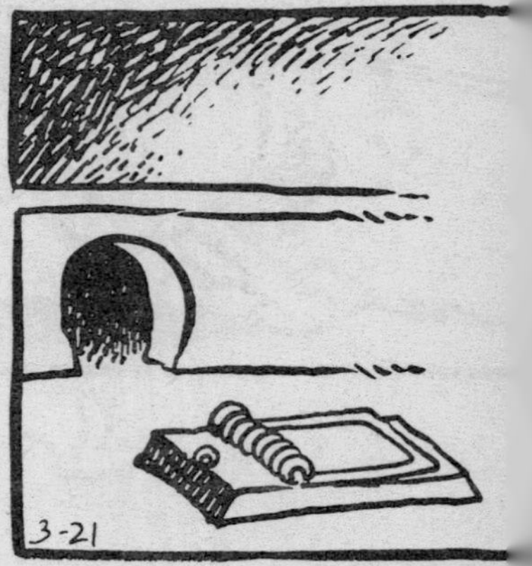
3-21

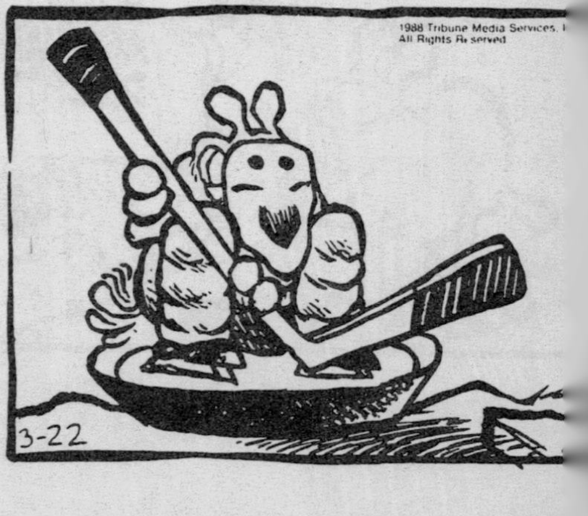
1988 Tribune Media Services, I
All Rights Reserved
3-22

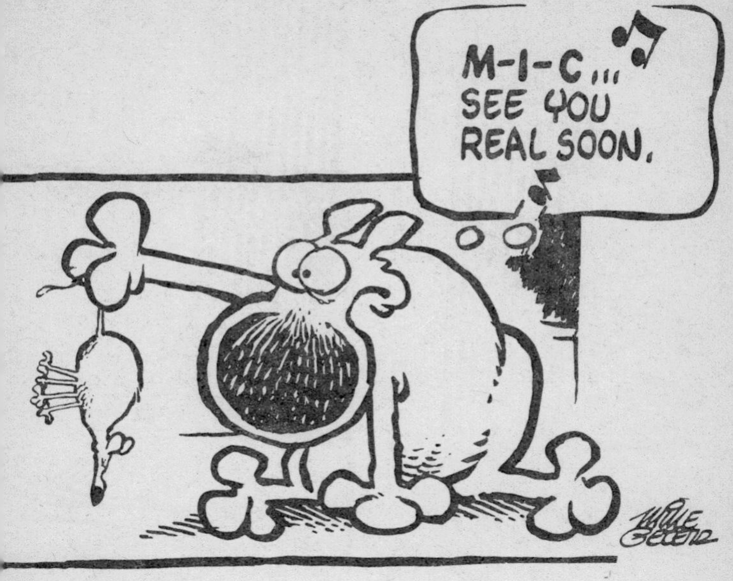
M-I-C...
SEE YOU
REAL SOON.
MIKE
PETERS

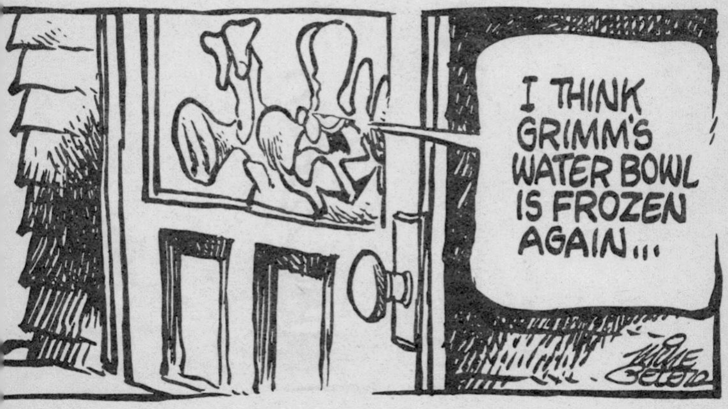
I THINK
GRIMM'S
WATER BOWL
IS FROZEN
AGAIN...
MIKE
PETERS